THE UNITED STATES
AND EASTERN EUROPE

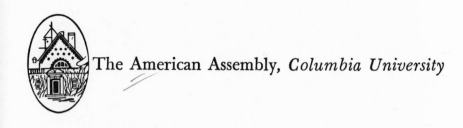

The American Assembly, *Columbia University*

THE UNITED STATES
AND EASTERN EUROPE

Prentice-Hall, Inc., *Englewood Cliffs, N. J.*

54264

Preface

Editor Robert F. Byrnes of Indiana University has stated that although there has been a recent awakening of interest, the general ignorance concerning Eastern Europe is colossal. This volume is intended to put into historical perspective some basic facts that Americans must take into account when considering policies and positions in our relations—social, political, economic—with the countries of Eastern Europe.

In the chapters which follow, *Eastern Europe* refers to the communist countries of Europe, exclusive of the Soviet Union—namely Poland, Romania, Czechoslovakia, Hungary, Bulgaria, Yugoslavia, East Germany and Albania. The authors describe the many diversities and complexities within and among these countries and set the background for American Assembly meetings on this subject throughout the United States.

The first of these meetings—the Thirty-first American Assembly—was held at Arden House, the Harriman (N.Y.) campus of Columbia University, in April 1967. The final report of that meeting, a statement of findings and conclusions for United States policy, may be had from The American Assembly.

The views contained herein are those of the writers and not necessarily of The American Assembly, a nonpartisan educational organization which takes no position on matters it presents for public discussion. Similarly, The Ford Foundation, which generously supported the entire American Assembly program on Eastern Europe, is not to be associated with the opinions reflected in the individual chapters.

Clifford C. Nelson
President
The American Assembly

ERRATUM

The United States and Eastern Europe (1st printing)

Page 22, second paragraph, line 12, which reads:

"gary than in Britain and Germany. National income per head in each"

should read:

"gary than in the Balkans. In the last ten years before the World"

11/67

Table of Contents

THE UNITED STATES
AND EASTERN EUROPE

Robert F. Byrnes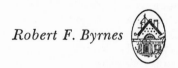

Introduction

Since the end of the Second World War and the transformation of Eastern Europe into territory controlled by Communists, American scholars and statesmen have debated concerning the term which should be applied to this area. For many, Eastern Europe is inaccurate and suggests that Prague and Warsaw are less European than is Vienna. They would therefore prefer the term East Central Europe to describe that territory now ruled by Communists between Germany, Austria, and Italy on the west and the Soviet Union of the east. This disagreement is and has been an important one, because it reflects discussion concerning the position of the people of this area in the culture, the past, and the future of Europe. In this volume, Eastern Europe has been chosen because the term is clear and accurate and is also more widely accepted than is East Central Europe.

In any case, the term Eastern Europe itself is laden with significant dangers, largely because it suggests that the peoples and the countries of the area share a common history, tradition, and pur-

ROBERT F. BYRNES *is professor of history at Indiana University. He has written numerous books and articles on France, Russia, and Eastern Europe and has served the American government during the Second World War and the Korean War. Since 1955, he has helped to negotiate and to administer important academic exchanges with the Soviet Union and several of the countries of Eastern Europe as chairman for most of that time of the Inter-University Committee.*

pose. One of the principal contributions of the essays in this volume is the clear and succinct way in which they describe the extraordinary diversities which exist within many of these countries and among them as well. Poland is as close to Sweden in its history and culture as it is to Bulgaria. The Czechs are as different from the Romanians as they are from the Spanish, and the Germans and the Albanians as different as the Norwegians and the Greeks. In short, we should not consider Eastern Europe a unity or whole.

The enormous diversities within the area force the conclusion that there is no simple or single solution for the problems which face the lively and vital peoples who live there. Indeed, one of the purposes of this volume is to describe the complexities which these countries and peoples pose for everyone interested in their welfare and in the common weal.

The ignorance of the American people concerning Eastern Europe is colossal, in spite of the expansion of interest and knowledge concerning it in recent decades. It must be admitted that Eastern Europeans, for some of the same reasons, are markedly ignorant concerning the history and character of the United States, even though their interest in us has been high in the twentieth century. Our educational systems, until after the Second World War, almost totally neglected Eastern Europe, and most Americans have been led to believe that it was a backward and uncultured part of the world inhabited by strange people who used curious languages and had odd habits and customs. Indeed, few American universities in 1940 and 1945 taught any of the languages of this area or offered courses on the history or literature of the peoples of a central part of the world community. Our ignorance and our general failure to understand these peoples were contributory factors to the failures of American policy during and after the Second World War, as they were to our inability to help Europe and the world resolve the problems which faced us all at the close of the First World War.

Eastern Europe was, and will remain, a critical area of the world. It is an essential part of Europe, still one of the centers of world culture, of economic and military power, and of political and intellectual vitality. It contains more than 120,000,000 people, including some of the most lively and talented in the world. It has impressive resources of skilled manpower, growing industrial capacity, significant agricultural potential, and large stores of critical raw materials. It also stands at a vital strategic position in Europe and the world. Its history is studded with internal wars which exploded beyond its borders and with the efforts of outsiders, the Russians and the Turks and the Germans, to acquire control.

Since the end of the Second World War, the entire area, with the exception of Yugoslavia and Albania, has been under the direct influence and perhaps control of the Soviet Union. Soviet authority in Eastern Europe has provided the Soviet Union significant buffers for its frontiers. It has enabled the Soviet armed forces to establish bases removed from Soviet soil. It has added the resources of the area to those of the Soviet Union. It has enabled the Russians to maintain the division of Europe, provided the Soviet Union a veto concerning the unification of Germany, placed all of Western Europe under considerable military pressure and on occasion of direct military threat, and created among many Communists and non-Communists alike the fear that communism may in fact represent the wave of the future.

The fall of the countries of Eastern Europe from precarious independent rule in the 1930's to the position they have had since 1945 is one of the principal elements in the crisis which has afflicted the world. The unification of Germany and the acquisition by the peoples of Eastern Europe of control of their own political systems and of their foreign policies remain among the most delicate and dangerous problems now facing the world. Moreover, many of the issues which confront the peoples of Eastern Europe resemble those to which many other peoples must respond in the last third of the twentieth century. The mastery of what is commonly called modernization, the development of political and social systems which resolve pressing and permanent human needs, and the establishment of some balance between nationalism and regionalism in such a way as to produce world order—these and other major issues are models of what many peoples, and the United States in its policies, must face and resolve.

The volume is of particular significance because visible changes of great depth and power have been unfolding in Eastern Europe, the Soviet Union, and the international Communist movement since 1956. One might call the process as it affects Eastern Europe the unbinding of Soviet control over the area in a long and gradual process which may ultimately come to resemble what scholars in the nineteenth century called the Eastern Question. The new social and economic forces now operating in Eastern Europe, the impact of external changes, particularly the vitality of Western Europe, and shifting Soviet policies are some of the most important elements which will affect all of world politics in the last third of the twentieth century.

In short, this volume fits responsibly into The American Assembly series, which provide the basic facts in historical framework and perspective concerning critical problems facing the American people. It seeks to identify the principal issues at a critical time, to provide the informed reader the necessary background, and to suggest policies and positions which the American people must consider before they reach their final decisions.

The essays in this volume have been written by outstanding American scholars who combine the range of knowledge and the objectivity associated with the academic community with the practical experience in dealing with the entire area and with the main issues outlined. The maps were generously and skillfully provided by Professor Norman J. G. Pounds of Indiana University. Two of the eight participating scholars were born in Eastern Europe, one in Germany, one in England, and four are native Americans. Thus, the origins of the authors, their qualities, and their experiences reflect a part of the American heritage, which has been woven by peoples from all parts of the world, including that area which is the subject of this volume.

Stephen D. Kertesz

1

The Land and Peoples in History

AREA

The history of Eastern Europe has been shaped to a large extent by its geography. It lies between the Baltic, Adriatic, Black, and Aegean Seas and divides roughly into three major geographic regions: the Baltic area, the mid-Danubian depression or Carpathian basin, and the Balkans. The Baltic area forms a region 300 miles in breadth between the Carpathians and the Baltic Sea, is part of the North European plain, and gives easy access to the almost endless Russian steppes and to Western Europe. The openness of the area has influenced the fate of the Polish and Baltic nations. It was one of the highways of traditional German expansion eastward. Since the eighteenth century, Russian armies have marched westward through the same route.

The mid-Danubian depression is defended in the east and north by the solid arch of the Carpathian mountains, crossed by major armies only three times after the establishment of the Hungarian state in the tenth century. However, the same area is open from the

STEPHEN D. KERTESZ *had a distinguished diplomatic and scholarly career in his native Hungary. He was Secretary General of the Hungarian Peace Delegation to the Conference of Paris in 1946 and Hungarian Minister to Italy in 1947. Since 1951 he has been Professor of Political Science at the University of Notre Dame. He is the author or editor of eight books and numerous articles on international political affairs.*

west and south; the Danube has long been an artery of communication between the German lands and the Balkan countries.

The Balkan peninsula lies open from the north. Invasion from the south is not easy, although the Ottoman Turks accomplished this feat and occupied most of the Balkan peninsula for more than four centuries. Modern Turkey still controls the Bosporus and Dardanelles and in eastern Thrace retains a foothold on European soil. The Balkan peninsula is dominated by rugged and disorderly mountain ranges which divide the peninsula in different directions and hamper political unification.

Eastern Europe as a whole is geographically an amorphous region whose boundaries both on the east and on the west are neither hard nor fast and have been subject to dramatic changes. It is sometimes called the borderland of Western civilization. The dividing line between Western and Eastern Europe changed often during the last two thousand years. The Roman *limes,* the boundary of the Old Roman Empire, was established for centuries roughly along the Rhine and Danube, and included the Balkan peninsula. However, the incursions of the barbarian tribes, the collapse of Rome, the great age and decline of Byzantium, settlement of Slavic and other peoples, national victories and catastrophes, invasions, and Ottoman rule of the Balkan peninsula have produced continued shifting of the boundary between Eastern and Western Europe. Even so, despite constant change throughout history, there has been a continuous European tradition in most East European countries, for the European idea, like Western civilization, is not primarily a geographic concept. It is connected with the way of life, the institutions, and the values of a larger Europe in which most East Europeans have an ineradicable sense of participation.

RECENT TERRITORIAL CHANGES

The Nazi-Soviet cooperation and the Second World War brought many changes and made possible the westward expansion of the Soviet Empire. In 1945, Western Europe faced the *Pax Sovietica* along the line running from Lubeck to Trieste. Moscow installed Communist regimes in the countries east of this line and erected the iron curtain which separated Eastern and Western Europe and interrupted relations which had been shaped by a thousand years of history. In Northeastern Europe, the Soviet Union annexed Lithuania, Latvia, Estonia, and some parts of Finland and East Prussia, Romania ceded Bessarabia and part of Bukovina, and Czechoslovakia ceded Ruthenia to the Soviet Union. The most important territorial change was the westward shift of the Polish state. Poland lost nearly half of her prewar territory to the Soviet Union. Although she received compensation in the West (still not sanctioned by a peace treaty), the present area of Poland is smaller by 20 per cent than it was in 1938.

The peace treaties signed in 1947 made some other territorial changes. Czechoslovakia obtained three villages from Hungary, and Italy ceded Istria, Zadar and some Adriatic islands to Yugoslavia. The Trieste question was settled in 1954. Bulgaria was allowed to keep southern Dobrudja, annexed in 1940. The Soviet Government in 1949 organized in the part of Germany occupied by Soviet troops the so-called German Democratic Republic, a new state virtually without precedent in German history.

PEOPLES

This volume considers that Poland, Eastern Germany, Czechoslovakia, Hungary, Romania, Bulgaria, Yugoslavia, and Albania together constitute Eastern Europe. The territory of these eight states totals 492,000 square miles with a population of more than 120 million. (The combined area of Texas, New Mexico and Colorado is 493,252 square miles.) Although Greece is part of the Balkan peninsula, the Greek nation is more Mediterranean than East European.

The population of the eight Eastern European states under consideration is heterogeneous. With the exception of the Albanians, Romanians, Hungarians (Magyars), and Germans, the inhabitants of the area are Slavs. The Bulgars, Serbs, Macedonians, Croats, and Slovenes are Southern Slavs, and the Poles, Czechs, and Slovaks are Western Slavs. Some of these peoples have played a considerable political and cultural role in Europe over the centuries, but knowledge about them is vague in Western countries.

It is impossible to obtain entirely reliable data on the ethnic and religious situation in Eastern Europe today, because the statistics are influenced by various political considerations. Some states, notably Poland, East Germany, Albania, and Hungary have few national minorities. Others remain multi-national states. In Yugoslavia, the mosaic of nationalities has changed little since 1918. The Serbs, Croats, Slovenes, Macedonians and Montenegrins form the national majority, but there are almost a million Albanians, over half a million Hungarians, and about 600,000 from other nationalities. In Romania, there are 1,600,000 Hungarians, almost 400,000 Germans, and over 500,000 from other minorities. Czechoslovakia contains 580,000 Hungarians and 333,000 from other minorities.

Although most East European countries have not published statistics on religious affiliation since the Second World War, it is clear that the overwhelming majority of the Poles, Slovenes, and Croats, and a large majority of the Czechs, Slovaks and Hungarians are Roman Catholics, although there are important Protestant groups in Bohemia, Slovakia and Hungary. The Greek Catholic Church, or Uniate Church, was liquidated in Poland and Romania. The Serbs, Macedonians, Montenegrins, Bulgarians and Romanians are overwhelmingly Greek Orthodox. The majority of Albanians are Moslems; 20 per cent of them are Greek Orthodox, and 10 per cent Roman Catholic. In Yugoslavia, there are over two million Moslems, and in Bulgaria over 800,000.

Major historical events have profoundly affected the ethnic composition of the Eastern European countries. Nationalism, of course, did not exist in the modern sense before the French Revolution and immigrants were considered assets. Thus, the first Hungarian king, St. Stephen, admonished his son that a country of only one language is weak. For centuries, the Polish, Bohemian, and Hungarian kings welcomed German settlers. In addition to peaceful German expansion in Eastern Europe, the Teutonic Knights conquered and Germanized large territories along the Baltic, where Germans belonged to the dominant social class until 1918. In Southeastern Europe, the Turkish occupation greatly contributed to the ethnic complexity. Eastern Europe tended to become the home of small nations sandwiched between overwhelming outside forces which contended for control of the area. Indigenous East European states seldom could establish a Great Power position. When any of them succeeded, the result was a multi-national state.

The Balkan Wars (1912–1913) and the two World Wars were followed by large scale population movements. Between 1912 and 1937, over 700,000 Turks moved from the Balkan countries to Turkey. Austria-Hungary was dismembered in the name of the principle of nationality, but self-determination was not applied to Germans, Hungarians or Bulgars. The result was a substantial exodus.

The Second World War saw a large-scale destruction of the Jewish population and a drastic reduction of the German population in Eastern Europe. During the 1939–41 period of cooperation between Berlin and Moscow, Hitler repatriated the Germans from the Baltic states, Bessarabia, the Soviet-occupied parts of Poland and other East European regions. During the ensuing war, most Jews from Germany and from countries under German occupation were deported to the east, and about six million of them were murdered. Several million Poles from German or German-held provinces were deported. In the last stage of the war, many Germans from Eastern European countries sought refuge in Western Germany. At Potsdam in July, 1945, the British, United States and Soviet governments recognized that "the transfer to Germany of German populations, or elements thereof, remaining in Poland, Czechoslovakia and Hungary, will have to be undertaken." As a result, nearly 25 per cent of the present-day population of the Federal Republic of Germany consists of expellees and refugees from Eastern Europe, about thirteen million persons in all. According to German statistics, 3.2 million Germans died or disappeared during the forced transfers.

The Potsdam Conference did not authorize the transfer of Hungarians, but the Czechoslovak government sought to achieve this end by discriminatory legislative measures and forced expulsion. Eventually, under Soviet pressure, in February, 1946, Hungary signed a population exchange agreement with Czechoslovakia. Persons of Slovak or Czech ethnic origin could transfer at will from Hungary to Czechoslovakia, while the government in Prague could select an equal number of Hungarians for transfer to Hungary. Altogether, 92,000 Hungarians were expatriated or expelled from Czechoslovakia to Hungary and 60,000 Slovaks moved voluntarily from Hungary to Czechoslovakia.

Internal and External Forces

Historically speaking, the Eastern European nations have had two basic political problems. One is the lack of cooperation among themselves, often the result of exaggerated nationalism, and the other is their relationship with overwhelming outside forces. Both problems have been complicated by the interplay of complex ethnic and religious factors, and by intricate historical feuds.

The major outside forces were in the south Byzantium and later the Ottoman Empire, in the southwest Venice and Italy, in the west the various German states and on some occasions France, in the east the Tatars and other intruders, and since the twentieth century, the increasing power of Russia. Britain's continental

policy manifested interest in the smaller nations of Eastern Europe;
it concentrated on Western Europe and Russia. To the United
States, Eastern Europe seemed a faraway region, remote from the
national interest. This view prevailed even during the Second
World War, when the Joint Chiefs of Staff ruled that the United

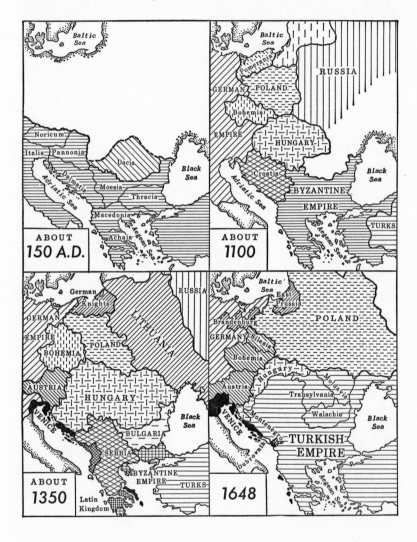

States should take no responsibilities "in the area of the Balkans, including Austria."

Recurring invasions have influenced the fate of the East European nations. On occasion, the East European nations fought together against Byzantine, Venetian, Tatar, Turkish, German or Russian armies. Most of the East European peoples had heroic periods and difficult periods as well. They like to recall national greatness, but national tragedies have also become parts of popular folklore. Historical feuds have also remained important, presenting opportunities to outside powers to play the East European nations against each other. It is not by accident that the sparks igniting both world wars were struck in Eastern Europe.

The system of small states established in Eastern Europe after the First World War was exceptional. During the last one-thousand years, either indigenous powers brought several nations together under one rule, or the East European peoples were included in the imperial domains of outside powers. Thus, the Balkan nations lived as subjects of the Ottoman Empire for almost five centuries. Croatia was an associated state of Hungary from 1102 to 1918; territories inhabited by Slovenes were parts of Austria for twelve centuries. After the Battle of Mohács in 1526, the Croatian and Hungarian regions not occupied by the Turks became parts of the Hapsburg Empire. At the time America was discovered, the Polish-Lithuanian Commonwealth was the largest European state and included Poles, Lithuanians, Ukrainians, White Russians, Jews, and other ethnic groups. By the end of the eighteenth century, after the final partition of Poland, the Poles lived in Prussia, Austria and Russia. The historical maps sufficiently illustrate these developments.

Early History

EMERGENCE OF NATIONAL KINGDOMS

Roughly around the year 1,000 A.D. the nations of Eastern Europe began to emerge as cultural, if not political entities. Croatia, Hungary, Bohemia, and Poland became Catholic kingdoms, while Kievan Russia, Bulgaria, and Serbia accepted under Byzantine influence the Greek Orthodox version of Christianity. The Bulgarians and Serbs established their states in the central and eastern regions of the Balkan peninsula. Dazzled by Byzantium, the great Bulgarian and Serb rulers tried to conquer Constantinople in the periods of weak-

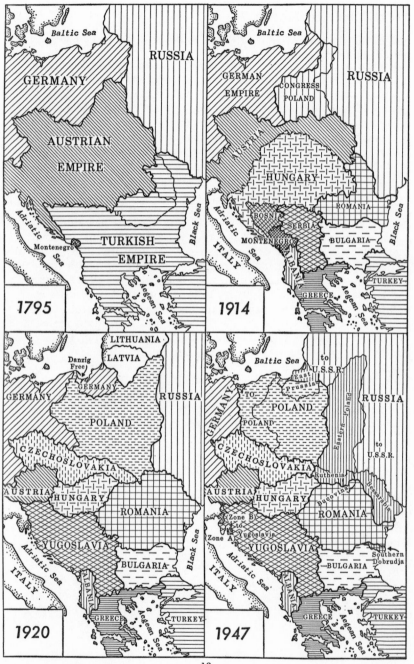

ness of the Empire. After they failed, both countries lived for some periods under Byzantine rule.

It is interesting to note at this point the far-reaching effect of some early historical events in the Balkans. The Roman Empire was divided into an Eastern and a Western part in 395 A.D., and the line of this division followed roughly the Drina River to the Sava and to the Danube. This line divided the ecclesiastical jurisdictions of Rome and Constantinople, and eventually became the frontier between Roman Catholics and Greek Orthodox. Although this frontier changed little throughout history, during the Ottoman rule the Orthodox Serbs expanded to the north and west. The religious division had far-reaching political consequences, best illustrated by the chasm still existing in Yugoslavia between the Catholic Slovenes and Croats and the Orthodox Serbs. The Slovenes and Croats have become substantially Western in their outlook. Common religion and similar political institutions greatly facilitated cooperation between Croats and Hungarians until the advent of modern nationalism. North of the Carpathians, Poland formed a bulwark of western Christianity. To the northwest, Bohemia played an important role in Central European politics. East and south of Hungary, the Orthodox world began.

The history of these three Catholic Kingdoms, Poland, Bohemia, and Hungary, was similar, although their fate differed, largely because of geography. Poland and Hungary were "border states" between East and West; unlike Bohemia, neither became a member of the Holy Roman Empire. The "golden age" of Bohemian history was the rule of Emperor Charles IV (1347–1378), when Bohemia was given first place among the empire's secular electors and Prague became one of the chief cities of the Empire. Prague was the first city in the north where a university was established and humanism flourished. Reform movements began in the Church, which culminated in the activities of John Hus. Although the Council of Constance decided to burn him as a heretic, his ideas survived and the Hussite movement became a forerunner of the Reformation. The era of progress and reforms came to an end at the Battle of White Mountain in 1620, when Hapsburg Ferdinand II defeated the Czech army, and Bohemia became a province of the Hapsburg Empire.

From the eleventh to the sixteenth century, Hungary, Bohemia, and Poland enjoyed generally favorable developments. The Tatars devastated Poland and Hungary in 1241–42, but then retreated because of the death of the Great Khan. However, the Tatars de-

stroyed Kievan Russia, and most parts of Russia remained under
their rule or influence for two centuries and more. During the Tatar
domination, almost all political relations between Russia and Europe
were severed. This situation greatly influenced developments in
Eastern Europe; while Russia withered under Tatar isolation,
Poland and Lithuania, united under the same ruling family,
achieved a period of political and cultural greatness. Renaissance
scholarship and art flourished in the Polish-Lithuanian Commonwealth, the largest and most powerful country in Eastern Europe,
and constitutional developments advanced rapidly.

During the Renaissance, the three East European kingdoms and
Austria participated in the great revival of arts and letters and the
systematic organization of scholarly studies. The universities established in Prague (1348), Cracow (1364), and Vienna (1365), became
celebrated centers of learning. Hungary then had four university
foundations, in Pécs (1367), Old Buda (1397), Pozsony (1465), and
Buda (1475), but these had a more precarious existence and disappeared amidst political adversities.

OTTOMAN CONQUEST AND RULE

After a long era of favorable political, economic and cultural developments, Hungary and Bohemia suffered a decline of political
and social leadership, which facilitated the advance of the Ottoman
Turks toward Central Europe. The Turks came from Asia Minor
and entered the Balkan peninsula in the fourteenth century. They
subdued Bulgaria and Serbia and gradually advanced toward present-day Belgrade. In the fifteenth century, the Ottoman Empire
reached the Danube and Sava rivers and consolidated its rule in the
lower Danube valley. After the capture of Constantinople in 1453,
the Sultan attacked the fortress of Belgrade, then a Hungarian out-
post. The Turks were repelled from Belgrade, but they conquered
Bosnia, Albania, Herzegovina, and the Romanian principalities,
Wallachia and Moldavia.

Suleiman the Magnificent took Belgrade in 1521, attacked Hungary, and killed Louis Jagiello, king of Hungary and Bohemia, in
the fateful battle of Mohács in 1526. The Hapsburg family then
inherited both the Bohemian and the Hungarian thrones, until
1918. Another consequence of the battle of Mohács was the Turkish
occupation of two-thirds of Hungary.

The Ottoman Empire in a sense continued Byzantine politics in
the Balkan peninsula, and had a lasting effect on political and

cultural developments there. The Orthodox Church remained dominant in the Balkans; the Turks seldom trusted Catholics because of their permanent link with Rome, but the Orthodox Church was not only tolerated but became an active participant in the administration and power structure of the Ottoman Empire. The majority of Albanians were converted to Islam, and substantial conversions took place in Bosnia and Bulgaria also. The Balkan nations were subjected during long periods to exploitation; during the decaying centuries of the Ottoman Empire, they suffered under particularly corrupt administration. Even during periods of formal peace, hostilities continued between the Ottoman and Hapsburg armies in peripheral regions. The northern boundary of the Ottoman Empire fluctuated. Wars were fought mostly in the plains and on the hillsides, mainly populated by Hungarians and Croats. Centers of culture were annihilated, and the ethnic composition of these regions drastically changed.

East of the Carpathians, Poland fought bloody wars with the Turks. In the Balkans, tiny Montenegro was the only country which could maintain a precarious independence during the centuries of Turkish rule. On the Dalmatian coast, the city of Dubrovnik (Ragusa) enjoyed autonomy and became important in international trade. It played the role of a Hong Kong between the Ottoman Empire and the West.

HUNGARY AND TRANSYLVANIA

Historic Hungary was divided into three parts: the central area, the great Hungarian Lowland, which became a Turkish province; upper and western Hungary with Croatia, which were under Hapsburg rule; and Transylvania, which subsisted as a semi-independent principality (1541–1690) mostly tributary to the Sultan, but owing allegiance sometimes to the Emperor. The Hapsburgs made attempts to recover Transylvania, but these efforts failed until the end of the seventeenth century. Some of the Transylvanian princes took an active part in European diplomacy, particularly during the wars of religion. They maintained close relations and sometimes concluded alliances with Western European Protestant powers and with France to strengthen their position against the Hapsburgs. In the second part of the seventeenth century, Transylvania was ravaged by Turkish and Tatar invasions, and gradually disappeared as a power factor from the European scene.

The liberation of Hungary was probably the last crusade of Christendom. The fortress of Buda was reconquered from the Turks in 1686 by an international army, in which nearly all European nations were represented. Within thirty years, all of Hungary was set free. The ceded territories had been devastated and depopulated, and the Vienna government ordered a large-scale colonization effort. Settlers were invited from all over Europe; most of them came from German lands. Refugees from the Balkans, mainly Serbs and Romanians, were welcomed. Foreigners were granted huge properties in the liberated territories. Transylvania and some districts in southern Hungary along the Turkish boundary were organized as a separate unit called the Military Frontier, and governed directly from Vienna. Under King Mathias, at the end of the fifteenth century, Hungary had possessed a population of approximately five million, the large majority of which was Magyar. A census in 1720 revealed three and one half million persons in Hungary proper. The proportion of the Magyars drastically diminished.

The Hapsburgs and Russia

Between the sixteenth century and the First World War, the Hapsburg Empire acquired new territories, became a great power in Eastern Europe, and constituted one of the pillars of the European system. While its position was no longer threatened from the Balkan peninsula, two formidable outside forces emerged to compete for supremacy in Eastern Europe, Russia and Germany.

As the Tatar power withered away, the Muscovite position became greatly strengthened and Russia began a policy of unification and expansion. When Peter the Great defeated Sweden, Russia gained the Baltic provinces, a "window to the West," and became a great power. The Russians continued to expand westward, at first with Austria's help against Prussia, Poland, and Turkey. Late in the eighteenth century Russia made a fundamental change in her diplomacy, shifting to close collaboration with Prussia, which lasted until 1890, with the exception of the years from 1789 to 1812.

POLAND'S FATE

The most important results of the Russian policy of expansion were the three partitions of Poland in 1772, 1793, and 1795, which obliterated Poland and made Russia a neighbor of both Austria and Prussia. Poland's fate raised a general problem. Can a freedom-loving and decentralized country effectively resist centralized and tightly governed autocracies? In Poland, "golden freedom" flourished for many generations, and the Poles were quite effective in fighting for their country. Their love for freedom culminated in the acceptance of the unanimity rule in the Polish Diet in 1652, which prevented action unless every single member of the legislature agreed. The unanimity rule and the decline of social responsibility began to paralyze political development. After the last strong Polish king, John Sobieski, who helped defeat the Turks at Vienna in 1683, the Polish nobility was unwilling to elect a strong ruler and often yielded to foreign pressure in the elections of the king. Poland was also weakened by wars fought against the Germans, Turks, Russians, and Cossacks, but the deterioration of political and social conditions was decisive in her fall. Pro-German and pro-Russian groups of the nobility were manipulated by outside forces, and Poland became a pawn in Russian, Prussian, Swedish, and Austrian politics.

RUSSIAN EXPANSION

Shortly after Poland's partition, Russia demonstrated outstanding military power by playing a decisive role in the Napoleonic wars; subsequently, Russia became a leading power of the Quadruple Alliance, and later, as a member of the Concert of Europe along with Prussia and Austria, served as a bulwark of European conservatism. Intervention against the forces of revolution and territorial expansion characterized the foreign policy of the tsars in the nineteenth century, at the expense of the tottering Ottoman Empire and also in Central Asia and in the Far East. The treaty of Kuchuk Kainardji in 1774 gave Russia the right to protect Orthodox Christians in the Ottoman Empire, thus providing a pretext for intervention in the Balkans. Russia on occasion displayed a crusading spirit for the liberation of Orthodox Christians and fought repeated wars against the Ottoman Empire, with the objective of these wars control of the Balkan peninsula and the Straits. Russian endeavors to expand in Eastern Europe and Western resistance thereto created the Eastern Question. Russian expansion was greatly slowed by Western opposition, and German diplomacy later tried to divert Russia's attention from Europe by encouraging expansion in the Middle and Far East.

THE HAPSBURG LANDS

The chief organizing force in Central Eastern Europe, the Austrian Empire, was a multi-national state. Its citizens were greatly affected by the ideas of the French revolution, especially by a great driving force of modern times, nationalism. In addition, the ideas of German romanticism had a powerful effect on most East European nations and strengthened national movements.

The growth of nationalism in Hungary began with the use of the vernacular. Until the early nineteenth century, Latin was the official language of administration. The Diet in 1790–1791 introduced the teaching of Hungarian in schools and in 1830 enacted a law requiring officials to know the Magyar language. In 1844, Magyar replaced Latin altogether, and became the exclusive language of the legislature and administration. This development antagonized all the other nationalities, who wanted to replace Latin with their own vernaculars. During the 1830's and 1840's, the Diet gradually transformed Hungary into a modern state. The Acts of 1848 swept away many remainders of feudalism and established a government responsible to parliament. The establishment of constitutional government, however, did not satisfy the national aspirations of the non-Magyar peoples in Hungary, nor could these reforms be tolerated by the absolutistic Austrian Empire. In this complex situation, Vienna became the ally of the non-Magyar nationalities against the Hungarian regime established under a liberal politician, Louis Kossuth. In the ensuing armed conflict, the Croats, Serbs, and Romanians turned against Kossuth's regime, which then issued a Declaration of Independence in April, 1849. Eventually Vienna, with the aid of a Russian army, crushed Hungarian independence. R. W. Seton-Watson suggested that the central tragedy of 1848 was the fact that the Magyars, who were the torchbearers of constitutional liberty in the Danubian countries, were at the same time advocates of ethnic uniformity and assimilation and tried to apply to the other ethnic groups the same methods which they so resented when applied by the Germans to them.

In the second half of the nineteenth century, the Slav nationalities of the Danubian empire received increasing help and encouragement from Russia, which saw them as a convenient vehicle for Russian influence. As the Turkish danger, which had created a common interest in defense among the peoples of the Monarchy disappeared, Holy Russia came to be considered by many of the Slavs as a benevolent "big brother," not a danger.

THE NATIONALITY PROBLEM

For a time during the 19th century, Austria in appearance at least made progress toward establishing stability in Eastern Europe. The

Compromise of 1867 established the system of the Dual Monarchy, placing the Kingdom of Hungary on a par with Austria. At the basis of this compromise was the establishment of three joint services, foreign policy, defense, and finance. A minister common to both countries was appointed to control each of the three ministries, and made responsible to delegations of the two countries, elected annually by their parliaments.

The dualist experiment failed because it hindered the development of federalism, which alone could have saved the monarchy and provided stability. The new constitution, which gave rule to the Germans and Hungarians, and the anachronistic structure of the Monarchy, caused growing dissatisfaction, particularly among the Slavs and the Romanians. Austria was a conglomeration of heterogeneous lands and peoples and in Hungary the nationalities had outnumbered the Magyars since liberation from Turkish rule. In both countries, attempts were made to settle the nationality problems, but none of them was successful. Thus, the conflict between the German and Czech population in Bohemia caused much trouble and none of the several experimental solutions satisfied either the Czech or the German inhabitants.

In Hungary, the Nationalities Law of 1868 was a liberal legislative measure, perhaps "one of the best nationality laws that has ever been drafted." However, the provisions of the law were only partly implemented, and the nationalities were not satisfied because the law guaranteed only individual rights to members of the various nationality groups and did not grant local autonomies or other corporate rights. Later, as genuine liberalism withered, the Hungarian government followed a policy of Magyarization, stimulated in part by the fact that the irredentist movements of the nationalities were supported abroad. The intransigence of Hungarian nationalism contributed to the weakening of the Monarchy and was an obstacle to all large-scale reforms along federative lines.

Hungarian nationalism was not a unique phenomenon in Eastern Europe, for some other governments were even more intransigent. The Poles were oppressed and subject to Germanization in Prussia and to Russification in Russia. They repeatedly revolted against Russia, Prussia, and Austria. After the Polish revolt of 1830–1831, the Tsar incorporated the "Kingdom of Poland"—a creation of the Vienna Congress—directly into Russia. A Polish uprising of 1863 failed and led to retaliatory measures and renewed efforts at Russification. The 1846 and 1848 revolts in Prussian Poland and Austrian Galicia were suppressed, and the Free City of Cracow was incorporated into Austria.

THE DECLINE OF THE CONCERT OF EUROPE

Corrosion of the Concert of Europe advanced rapidly. While oppressing Poles and Ukrainians, Russia simultaneously proclaimed herself the mother and liberator of the Slavs and encouraged the Slav national movements in the Balkans and in Austria-Hungary, one of the chief opponents of Russia's expansion into the Balkans. The Congress of Berlin in 1878 prevented the establishment of Russian preponderance in the Balkans and the creation of a great Bulgarian state which, under Russian protection, would have extended from the Black and Aegean Seas almost to the Adriatic. The compromise worked out in Berlin created dissatisfaction in most Balkan countries, particularly in Bulgaria. Bismarck succeeded in maintaining friendly relations with Russia, but the situation changed radically after his resignation in 1890. Increasing German influence in the Danubian and Balkan regions and the projected Berlin-Baghdad railway threatened British interests in the Middle East, and the German naval building program challenged British maritime supremacy on the high seas. Thus, German policy involuntarily helped reconcile the two traditional enemies of the nineteenth century, Britain and Russia. With the formation of the Triple Alliance and the Triple Entente, a rigid balance of power, a "two-power world," was created in Europe.

As Ottoman power declined, the Balkan states gradually regained their independence. The fight for liberation started with the Serb uprising in 1804 and ended with the liberation of Macedonia in the first Balkan war of 1912. Independence was achieved through a variety of processes. The independence of Serbia, Romania, and Montenegro was recognized in 1878 by the Congress of Berlin. In 1908 the Sultan recognized the full sovereignty of Bulgaria and in 1913, the London Conference of Ambassadors recognized Albania as a neutralized state under the protection of the Great Powers. The newly independent states found adjustment to the modern world a most difficult task. Economic and cultural backwardness and political instability remained. It is not easy to change corrupt and inefficient administrations. The heritage of Ottoman rule and competition by Russia, Austria-Hungary, Germany, and Italy for control over the Balkan states hampered progress and modernization. The Austro-Hungarian annexation of Bosnia-Herzegovina in 1908 created a further tension, which was aggravated by the two Balkan wars fought for territories of European Turkey. In the first war, a coalition consisting of Bulgaria, Serbia, Greece, and Montenegro defeated Turkey, but the victorious allies were unable to agree on the territorial settlement. This precipitated the second Balkan war, in which the joint forces of Serbia, Romania, Greece, and Turkey defeated Bulgaria and eliminated her territorial gains. Because of general dissatisfaction and increased Serbian ambitions, the Balkan powder keg was near explosion and the stage was set for the holocaust of World War I.

The First World War

Until 1918, Western statesmen considered the Danubian Empire a cornerstone of the European state system. According to the famous Czech historian, František Palacký, it would have been necessary to create the Hapsburg Monarchy if it had not existed. In the middle of the nineteenth century, Palacký proposed the transformation of the Monarchy into a federation in which all nationalities would enjoy equal rights and cooperate under a Hapsburg ruler. These ideas came later to be known as Austroslavism and gained wide acceptance. Even one of the chief advocates of the destruction of the Monarchy during the First World War, Eduard Beneš, stated prior to the war that he opposed the dismemberment of Austria because of the existence of powerful historic and economic bonds between the Austrian nations.

In the early stage of the World War, the Entente Powers did not plan the liquidation of Austria-Hungary. President Wilson stated in his address to the American Congress on December 4, 1917: "We do not wish in any way to impair or rearrange the Austro-Hungarian Empire. . . . We only desire to see that their affairs are left in their own hands in all matters, great or small." On January 5, 1918, Prime Minister Lloyd George stated that the British were not fighting to destroy Austria-Hungary and that a breakup of that Empire was no part of their war aims. However, the promises made in the course of the war to Italy, to Romania, and later to the other nationalities could not have been fulfilled without the destruction of the Monarchy. Moreover, in the last months of the war the propaganda and diplomatic activity of the Entente powers underwent a change with regard to the fate of Austria-Hungary. Some Western statesmen fell under the spell of their own wartime propaganda. During the last stage of the war, revolutionary movements in the Monarchy were encouraged from outside. The leaders of the various nationalities received encouragement, and even instructions from abroad. In this process, Czech political leaders in the western countries played a leading role, and the creation of Czechoslovakia was the decisive blow.

Although the Entente Powers originally did not plan to dismember Austria-Hungary nor otherwise to change the general structure of the European system, the war was followed by basic shifts of power. Austria-Hungary broke up into its constituent national elements, while both Germany and Russia temporarily ceased to be major powers. A positive result of the peace settlement was the re-establishment of Poland, but the eastern boundary of the new state was defined only by the Treaty of Riga in 1921.

The small successor states could not replace the political and economic power of the Danubian Empire. The European state system had been based on the coexistence of great powers, one of which was located in the strategically important East Central European area. The political structure of the Empire may have been obsolete but the 52 million inhabitants of the Monarchy could nonetheless trade freely over a greater territory than that of any other European state except Russia. The peoples of the Monarchy had a common currency, and a customs union. Since Vienna was an international financial center, one could obtain loans on more advantageous terms for industrial investments and other purposes in Austria-Hungary than in Britain and Germany. National income per head in each War, per capita money income rose in Austria by 86 per cent and in Hungary by 92 per cent; the increases of real income in the same period were 62 and 75 per cent. Indeed, the rate of improvement in living standards was much more rapid in Austria and Hungary than in Britain and Germany. National income per head in each of the successor states was considerably smaller between 1919 and 1938. Moreover, the Monarchy's dissolution fatally weakened the power structure of Europe. Winston Churchill was justified in calling the breakup of the Empire a "cardinal tragedy." The path lay open for a central European power to move toward the east or for an Eastern power to move toward Western Europe.

After 1918

The peace settlement shifted 38,000,000 of the 52,000,000 inhabitants of the Austro-Hungarian Monarchy into countries belonging to the victors. By virtue of the peace treaties of St. Germain and Trianon, the territory of Austria-Hungary was divided among Austria, Czechoslovakia, Yugoslavia, Italy, Hungary, Poland and Romania. The peace settlement made Hungary the most dissatisfied state in Eastern Europe with approximately 3 million Hungarians attached to neighboring states. The loss of historic frontiers, the discontent of 350,000 refugees, and the existence of large Hungarian minorities in adjacent states were the chief causes of irredentist movements in Hungary during the interwar years.

A summary by A. J. P. Taylor of the internal difficulties of Czechoslovakia and Yugoslavia reflects the problems all of the new states faced between the wars:

> Czechoslovakia and Yugoslavia, despite their national theory, reproduced the national complications of Austria-Hungary. Constitutional Austria had contained eight nationalities; Czechoslovakia contained seven. Great Hungary had contained seven nationalities; Yugoslavia contained nine. Czechoslovakia became a unitary state, in which the Czechs were "the people of the state," as the Germans had been in constitutional Austria. Yugoslavia had a period of sham federalism; then it too became a unitary state, which the Serbs claimed as their national state after the model of the Magyars in Hungary. . . .
>
> The Czechs could outplay the Slovaks; they could not satisfy them. Masaryk had hoped that the Czechs and the Slovaks would come together as the English and the Scotch had done; the Slovaks turned out to be the Irish. In the same way, the Serbs could master the Croats; they could not satisfy, nor even, being less skillful politicians, outplay them.

Some successor states inherited the complex nationality pattern of the Monarchy, but none possessed the fallen Monarchy's economic advantages. Dismemberment of the Monarchy was a flagrant contradiction to the world trend, which favored economic integration. The new settlement opened the door to political and economic nationalism on a scale hitherto unheard of. German and Magyar supremacy were wiped out, and in some countries the formerly oppressed peoples became the oppressors. The elaborate legislative and administrative measures of discrimination practiced by the successor states against national minorities especially in economic matters had been unknown in the Monarchy.

The organization of a democratic Central Eastern European federation should have been an important task at the peace conference. The peace-makers erred, not in providing these peoples the right of self-determination but in not insisting that they establish a union or federation which would have given them all the advantages of a great power and which would have been a strong factor toward peace and stability. The opportunity was unique, because the two major potential opponents of such a scheme, Germany and Russia, did not exist as power factors in 1919. The obstacles to the establishment of a politically integrated democratic federation were the extreme nationalism of the new states and lack of statesmanship. Most of the successor states, whether victorious or defeated, adopted the policy of an exaggerated protectionism, erecting high tariff walls and engaging, from time to time, in economic war.

The few vague endeavors towards economic cooperation which were made were not successful. Certain articles of the peace treaties opened the way for preferential trade agreements, but in the hostile political atmosphere these negotiations failed. André Tardieu's endeavors in 1932, which promised French financial assistance if the East European states concluded preferential trade agreements, also were fruitless. Cooperation in agriculture, between Yugoslavia, Romania and Hungary, proposed at the Bucharest Conference of 1930; the attempt at economic collaboration by Czechoslovakia, Romania, and Yugoslavia according to the provisions of an agreement reached in February, 1933; and the Rome Protocols signed by Austria, Hungary, and Italy in March, 1934—all were short-lived expedients and did not substitute for true economic collaboration.

Since the might of Germany and Russia existed as a potential even in the 1920's, some East European statesmen recognized the dangers inherent in the new order, or rather in the lack of order. Thus, in a speech delivered in April, 1926, Count Stephen Bethlen, Prime Minister of Hungary, declared:

> Today, we may not clearly realize that the small states formed from the territory of the late Monarchy may become eventually vassals of either Russia or Germany. As a result of the great struggle, not only the Monarchy has been cut to pieces, but also the Russian Empire has been torn by a violent revolution for a decade. Thus, fate has provided us with a breathing spell for the beginning of a new life. But how long is this state of affairs going to persist? There can be no doubt at all for a thinking man that the great Russian nation is going to become a factor in world politics sooner or later, and that the great German nation will also recuperate from its defeat.

Neither Hungary nor the other East European states used the "breathing spell" for constructive political purposes. In most of the successor states, retrograde political conditions and corruption reached a depth altogether unknown in the Monarchy. Police rule and even assassinations became general. In Yugoslavia, the leader of the Croat Peasant party, Stjepan Radić and four other Croat deputies, were shot while in a session of Parliament in June, 1928 by another member of Parliament who belonged to the Serb Radical Party. Political democracy remained meaningless to the masses, ruled by pseudo-parliamentary regimes or dictatorships. The West considered Czechoslovakia a notable exception. This country received the economic lion's share of the Monarchy, and considerable financial support from abroad. While balanced economic and social conditions facilitated the functioning of democratic political institutions, political democracy alone could not assure the independence of Czechoslovakia in the serious crises of 1938 and 1944–48.

Despite the existence of the League of Nations, which was intended by its creators to put an end to alliance-making diplomacy, alliances multiplied in interwar Eastern Europe. In the 1920's the only genuine great power on the old continent was France, and French diplomacy concentrated upon seeking security against Germany. France attempted to consolidate the new territorial settlement by alliance with Poland and by supporting the alliances concluded by Czechoslovakia, Yugoslavia and Romania, the Little Entente, against Hungarian revisionism. The Little Entente, the Balkan Entente, and an opposing Italo-Hungaro-Austrian combination could not survive the resurgent outside forces of Germany and the Soviet Union.

The double failure of the West in Eastern Europe was conspicuous. In the 1930's, France trusted the Maginot line and failed to support her East European allies against Nazi economic penetration and military conquest. The remilitarization of the Rhineland in 1936, the Nazi occupation of Austria in 1938, the liquidation of Czechoslovakia in 1939, and the lack of political determination in the West sealed the fate of Eastern Europe. After the defeat of Germany in 1945, the entire area became part of the Soviet security system. Only the presence of American military might in 1945 and later the North Atlantic Treaty organization prevented further Soviet expansion.

Eastern Europe under Russian control plays an ambivalent role. It is a threat to the security of the Western world, but it may also prove to be Achilles heel of the Soviet system. The people who live in this strategic area belong by history, tradition, and way of life to

Western or Mediterranean culture. The Soviet Union has been unable to absorb them, or even to make Communists of them. These nations have become transmission belts, so to speak, between Western Europe and the Soviet people, serving to introduce Western influences into the U.S.S.R. itself.

*   *   *

In the span of a single lifetime, the East European nations have witnessed the collapse of three domestic and international orders. In the course of these events, all the nationalities have committed errors and mistakes. These experiences suggest some solutions and the advantages of a great political and economic unit combined with the benefits of democratic equality, extended to all nationalities, would open the door to a better future. Modern technology and simultaneous cooperation with Western Europe and the Soviet Union should make possible the proper use of the natural resources, the talents, and the skilled manpower abundant in Eastern Europe. The difficulties are not insurmountable. National differences in Eastern Europe have been greatly exaggerated. For many centuries cooperation did take place. There is great similarity among Slavic languages of the area. Above all, the people possess similar culture, ways of living, and ideals. Large sections of the population would welcome a program of cooperation. Cleavages among the East European peoples have been created by an exaggerated interpretation of their historical traditions. Politicians with nothing to gain themselves from unity have frequently exploited national differences. Nationalist extremism is the most divisive force in Eastern Europe and plays into the hands of outside powers. Time and again, the Hapsburgs, the Nazis, and the Russians have exploited the conflicting national aspirations of the East Europeans for the promotion of their own interests.

History has demonstrated that small power nationalism does not work in the long run and that great-power imperialism is disastrous both to the East Europeans and to the whole of Europe. No Eastern European people wants to be incorporated in the Soviet system. Whatever sympathy existed for the Soviet system has evaporated because of the behavior of the occupying Soviet army, the imposition of an oppressive political system, and economic exploitation. For the last hundred years the East Europeans have compared their living conditions with Western European standards, and modernization meant and still means for the East Europeans catching up with Western countries.

The problems of Eastern Europe cannot be solved on the basis of narrow nationalism, and probably not at all within the boundaries of small national states. A better future must come from economic and political unification extending from the Baltic to the Aegean Sea. The Common Market and other international institutions in Western Europe offer patterns for collaboration. An East European federation could cooperate with the Soviet Union and be part of a new European system. If these small nations are unable to cooperate and achieve some unity among themselves, they will remain pawns in the hands of outside forces.

Alvin Z. Rubinstein

2

Politics and Political Change

That the political climate in Eastern Europe is changing is indisputable, but the implications of these changes for the Communist societies of Eastern Europe remain a matter of controversy and are central for the determination of United States policy toward Eastern Europe. The barometric readings vary from country to country and fluctuate over time, yet everywhere the indicators point to the erosion of Moscow's once unchallenged authority. At a time when the Soviet Union has overwhelming military power and impressive economic and technological achievement, Soviet political influence in the region between the Baltic and Black Seas is, paradoxically, no longer unquestioned nor absolute, as it was in the Stalin era. At a time when Soviet foreign policy has become global in its concerns and when Soviet influence in the non-Communist world is perhaps greater than ever before, Soviet authority within the Communist world has never been more questioned. The colossi of communism stand on the brink of an open diplomatic split, and the nations of Eastern Europe are seeking to gain for themselves ever wider measures of autonomy and additional options for the conduct of their domestic and foreign policies.

Nationalism is the principal force behind the pressure for change. After almost two decades of relative quiescence under Soviet

ALVIN Z. RUBINSTEIN *is professor of political science at the University of Pennsylvania. He has travelled extensively in Eastern Europe and the Soviet Union, and is the author of a number of books, including* Communist Political Systems, *and* The Soviets in International Organizations.

domination, East European nationalism is manifesting itself not only in the persistent attempts of local Communist Parties to acquire greater control over their own political systems, but also in their resistance to Moscow's efforts to reestablish its preeminence in bloc affairs, and in the indifference, suspicion, and animosity which they generally exhibit toward one another. A force still not sufficiently appreciated in the West, East European nationalism has given rise to developments which require a reassessment of the outer limits of political and economic autonomy which Moscow will accept in Eastern Europe.

The Transmutation of Soviet Authority

The uncertainty that has permeated Moscow's relationship with the East European countries in recent years is the consequence of a syndrome of schismatic developments: the post-Stalinist struggle for power in the Soviet Union and its effects on leadership rivalries and Party stability in Eastern Europe; Khrushchev's denunciation of Stalin at the Twentieth Congress of the Communist Party of the Soviet Union in February, 1956, and the advent of "destalinization," with its unforeseen release of disintegrative pressures; the desire of the Soviet leadership to establish relations with Eastern Europe on a less exploitative and more mutually beneficial basis; the emergence of fundamental policy and personality clashes between Moscow and Peiping to a degree inconceivable a few years ago and which now seem largely irreparable; Moscow's present preference for consensus rather than coercion in trying to advance alliance cohesion; the resurgence of Western Europe as a political and economic force in European affairs and the accompanying corrosion in Europe of Cold War attitudes and assumptions; and finally, the dramatic assertiveness of East European nationalism and the catalytic effect this is having on the internal evolution of the Communist political systems there. Cumulatively, these developments have wrought a fundamental change in Eastern Europe's relationship to the Soviet Union. Moscow, on its part, is bedeviled by doubts and indecision: how far can it go in tolerating East European wilfulness, opposition, and independent initiatives without jeopardizing its legitimate political and strategic interests in the area? The U.S.S.R.'s difficulties in maintaining a modicum of cohesion in its alliance system in Eastern Europe and in gaining acceptance for its views on the restructuring and strengthening of once subservient Eastern Europe may best be illustrated by examples taken from the military, economic, and political realms.

MILITARY AFFAIRS

The Warsaw Treaty Organization is the vehicle through which the Soviet Union assures its military and strategic control and seeks to maintain the military cohesion of the bloc. Established on May 14, 1955, the Warsaw Pact was designed to serve three main purposes: first, to provide a long-term juridical basis for the presence of Soviet troops in Eastern Europe; second, to facilitate the military integration of the Eastern European countries on a multilateral basis under the leadership of the Soviet Union; and third, to offset politically the inclusion of West Germany in NATO. Of late, Moscow has sought to infuse vitality and purposefulness into the alliance and to obtain greater commitments and cooperation from the East European members, but without success.

In July, 1966, at a meeting of the Warsaw Pact members convened in Bucharest, Soviet leaders pressed for increased financial commitments and integration of military commands. To the Soviet call for closer cooperation, the Romanians hinted that the time had come to put an "end to all blocs"; to Soviet rejoinders that the Warsaw Pact needed strengthening, Romanian officials reportedly commented, "We believe the Warsaw Pact is sufficiently strong to meet present needs"; to Soviet suggestions for the integration of military commands, the Romanians called for the rotation of command among the eight members—the Soviet Union, Poland, Czechoslovakia, East Germany, Hungary, Romania, Bulgaria, and Albania, which is still nominally a member—although command has heretofore always been vested in a Soviet citizen. The Romanians are adroitly aiming at a reduction of the Soviet military presence in Eastern Europe, in the expectation that this will further political autonomy. The Bucharest meeting highlighted the strains inevitable when the leader of an alliance system strives to maximize his military and political influence, while the small national constituents maneuver to place restraints on the authority of the Great Power, lest they find themselves unable to influence the decisions which will determine their fate.

THE POLITICAL FACTOR IN ECONOMIC INTEGRATION

A second example of Soviet frustration in promoting bloc cohesion may be seen in the field of economic cooperation. Romania has been the principal stumbling block here too, though Moscow has had difficulties also with others, notably Poland and East Germany. In the late 1950's, Khrushchev demonstrated considerable interest in promoting closer economic ties between the Soviet Union and the nations of Eastern Europe. After a number of delays due to pre-occupation with Soviet domestic problems, and against the back-ground of rapidly deteriorating relations with Communist China, Khrushchev in June 1962 published a lengthy essay in which he stressed the importance of economic integration and called for a "socialist division of labor" between Eastern Europe and the Soviet Union. Under the proposed arrangement, the economies of all mem-ber-nations would be transformed into an organic, unified, and mutually reinforcing entity, with each country undertaking to produce for the bloc those goods which it was particularly suited to produce at a comparative advantage. In this way, non-profitable, low-quality production would be eliminated and wasteful, duplica-tive investment ended.

To facilitate this grand economic design, COMECON (The Coun-cil for Mutual Economic Assistance) was to be made into a viable institution. Established in 1949 as a counter to the Marshall Plan, it was used by Stalin to exploit the East European economies and to keep them in economic bondage to the U.S.S.R. Though Poland and Czechoslovakia have applauded moves to infuse life into COMECON, Romania is at present opposed. At a lower level of economic development and industrialization than most of the East European countries, it refuses to accept the role of "a hewer of wood and a bearer of oil," to provide raw materials and foodstuffs for the other socialist countries while itself remaining under-indus-trialized. Furthermore, Romania fears that more extensive eco-nomic ties with the Soviet Union would only weaken its ability to maintain its present heady measure of political autonomy. A long and bitter experience with a covetous and callous neighboring colos-sus makes unlikely a sudden easing of anxieties and suspicions. Notwithstanding the rational quality of the Soviet arguments for closer economic cooperation, Romania now derides the notion of economic integration and the importance of COMECON. The Ro-manian position resembles that expressed by a derisive Hungarian joke: to signify their fraternity and sense of partnership, the COMECON countries wanted a common emblem; accordingly, they adopted a flag with a red field in which there are eight lean cows milking one another. As long as the implementation of COMECON recommendations requires unanimity, Moscow's attempt to establish a voluntaristic system operating under a supranational institutional umbrella must for the moment remain a chimerical aspiration. The primacy of political objectives precludes consensus on the terms of economic cooperation. Once again, as so often in Eastern Europe's history, political nationalism has overshadowed economic rationality.

THE INTERNATIONAL COMMUNIST CONFERENCE

Perhaps nowhere are the constraints on the exercise of Soviet authority in Eastern Europe more glaringly evident than in Moscow's repeated failure to command support for the convening of a conference of world Communist parties to denounce Peiping for its polemics and slanders against the Soviet Union, its unwillingness to mute the Sino-Soviet quarrel and close ranks behind North Vietnam, and its endangering of alleged international Communist unity. On a number of occasions, Moscow has utilized Hungarian and Bulgarian Communist leaders to propose such a conference. The suggestions have always failed. Few East European Communist Parties want a confrontation with the Chinese. Even those sympathetic to the Soviet position perceive that they derive tangible political benefits from continuation of the rift. Moscow has accepted, however grudgingly, greater domestic autonomy for the Eastern European countries in return for their backing in the Sino-Soviet dispute. The degree of support has varied over time, with some countries fluctuating between neutrality and unequivocal support. For example, until the fall of 1965, Poland tried to act as a conciliator. Failing in this, Poland tried to avoid an open decision until it finally firmly supported Moscow. Romania, on the other hand, has continued to maintain a neutral position, much to the annoyance of Moscow and the disappointment of Peiping. Both the Soviet Union and Communist China continue to court Romania, which has used the opportunity to earn for itself increased internal autonomy and a range of foreign policy options unequalled by any of the other members of the Warsaw Pact.

The diminution of Soviet domination can be assumed from the frequency with which Moscow's initiatives and preferences have been rejected: the Warsaw Treaty Organization remains powerful, but has not adopted Soviet proposals for reform or structural improvement in the machinery of the alliance; COMECON has been in the doldrums since 1964, and has little to show in supranational planning and investment, except for the 3,000 mile long *DRUZHBA* oil pipe-line providing Poland, Czechoslovakia, and East Germany with Soviet oil, and the electrical power grid linking the Soviet Union and several of the COMECON countries; and Eastern Europe is reluctant to support Moscow wholeheartedly against the Chinese. For fear of alienating the Poles, Czechs, and Hungarians, Moscow must tolerate Romanian and occasionally Polish obstructionism. The status quo seems preferable to the uncertainties entailed in promoting bloc multilateralism.

Continuity and Change in Communist Party Oligarchies

Few generalizations can be made about Eastern Europe. The region is a mosaic of peoples, traditions, and cultures, typified more by divergencies and mutual animosities than by similarities and friendships. Historically, Warsaw, Prague, Budapest, and Bucharest have been closer to Paris than to Moscow. In 1945, Soviet conquest and occupation wrought a forced change of orientation, and Communist Parties imposed new institutions, policies, and attitudes. With the exception of Yugoslavia, which pioneered its own road to national independence after being excommunicated from the Communist camp by Stalin in June, 1948, the nations of Eastern Europe were ruled until recently by Soviet-selected Communist satraps installed by the Red Army. They were kept in power by the Soviet Communist Party and compliantly cooperated in the harsh exploitation that characterized the period before Stalin's death in March, 1953. With few exceptions these East European Communist leaders rose to prominence in service of the Soviet political apparatus. Identified as "Muscovites" by their own people and lacking a base of popular acceptance in their own countries, they ruled through a combination of Soviet support and internal repression. Terror was used extensively to root out dissension; central planning and command economies were established to recast economic and social institutions in the Soviet image; power was concentrated in the hands of the "Muscovite" factions of the respective Communist Parties to ensure the primacy of Soviet interests and Party control; and administration of society was highly centralized, with control vested in the Kremlin's proconsuls.

For the variety of complex reasons noted previously, post-Stalin Soviet leaders began cautiously, often inadvertently, and finally reluctantly, to accept and cater to Eastern European nationalism.

Leadership changes occurred, sometimes dramatically as in Poland and Hungary in 1956, but more often slowly and behind the scenes. The trend was removal from power of the "Muscovites" and their replacement by "national Communists," i.e., by Communist officials who, generally speaking, had not compromised themselves in the eyes of their countrymen by slavish service to the Soviet Communist Party to the neglect of national needs and who sought to bring about a reduction of Soviet political and military "presence" and a reassertion of national prerogatives. The successes of the national Communists have been notable, particularly in the realm of foreign policy. Moscow can no longer command adherence to its wishes. To the extent that it seeks alliance solidarity on a particular issue, it must either persuade all or be hamstrung by the obstructionism of one of the nation-states of Eastern Europe.

The disproportionate attention Western commentators devote to Soviet-East European relationships in the realm of foreign policy should not obscure the important changes that have occurred within the political systems of these countries. These changes, however, defy any definitive or facile generalizations about the pattern of developments in the area as a whole. They differ from country to country, both in character and tempo, and they are not always consonant with initiatives in foreign policy. For example, Romania remains highly centralized and wedded to Stalinist institutions and constraints in industry and agriculture, notwithstanding its surprising defiance of Moscow's leadership in foreign affairs. On the other hand, Hungary generally supports Soviet foreign policy, but has liberalized its domestic situation considerably since 1957. Finally, Yugoslavia must be treated as a separate political phenomenon. Its level of decentralization and liberalization has already surpassed the most euphoric expectations of the position other Eastern European countries might attain in another decade if their reforms should take root and flourish. Yugoslavia remains Communist, but in a manner which engenders as much suspicion in the East as it does skepticism in the West.

LEADERSHIPS

The altered relationship between the nations of Eastern Europe and the Soviet Union has not affected the continued domination of these societies by elites whose power base is centered in the Communist Party. The Communist Party in each country remains the fulcrum of political power. It is in the executive organs of Communist

Parties that decisions are made regarding political and cultural life, the pace and direction of economic reform, and the manifold aspects of what is entailed under the rubric of modernization. The actual process by which decisions are reached is shrouded in secrecy, but the pattern of these policies is empirically observable: an end to the use of terror; a spectrum of open discussion and criticism of specific programs which extends from the remarkable candor heard in Yugoslavia to the controlled dialogue in Hungary to the unfathomable unanimity in Romania and Bulgaria; an easing of controls on the everyday life of the individual; and an attempt to set political parameters of what is permissible on a judicious basis.

Though there have been some shifts in the upper echelons of the Communist Parties, the key leaders have shown an unusual capacity for durability: Gomulka in Poland, Ulbricht in East Germany, Novotný in Czechoslovakia, Kadar in Hungary, Ceausescu in Romania, Zhivkov in Bulgaria, and Tito in Yugoslavia. However, the survivors from the Stalin era are gradually being replaced by new cadres, men whose loyalties are to their national Communist Party rather than to Moscow. The percentage of lower and middle echelon Communists trained in the Soviet Communist Party is diminishing. As the composition of the East European Communist Parties acquires an increasingly national and nationalistic character, it is reasonable to assume reinforcement of the evolving trend toward national autonomy.

However, the infusion of indigenously developed Party professionals does not involve any drastic diffusion of political power within the respective political systems. That the Party is *the* institution controlling the assignment of important posts is evident from even a cursory examination of the different countries. In Poland, Wladyslaw Gomulka, the First Secretary of the Polish United Workers (Communist) Party, does not hold a top government position, but clearly wields enormous authority. He announces major decisions and shapes Poland's foreign policy. When a new President had to be elected because of the sudden death of the incumbent in August, 1964, it was Gomulka who proposed Edward Ochab's name, thereby assuring unanimous reception by the compliant Parliament. The removal of Aleksander Ranković from his Party and governmental posts in July, 1966, was initially announced by the Central Committee of the Yugoslav Communist Party (League of Yugoslav Communists). In Hungary, Janos Kadar, the First Secretary of the Hungarian Socialist Workers (Communist) Party, determined the reshuffling of government positions after the elections in April, 1967.

Analysis of the Communist leaderships in Eastern Europe reveals that, thus far, a representative of the new generation of national Communists has risen to the top only in Romania. Nicolae Ceausescu has undramatically and efficiently impressed his authority upon the Romanian Communist Party since he assumed the post of Party Secretary in March, 1965, at the death of Gheorghe Gheorghiu-Dej. Young, colorless, able, he has skillfully advanced the policies of desovietization and Romanization introduced by Gheorghiu-Dej. The foreign policy features of desovietization have already been mentioned. Domestically, desovietization has resulted in the withdrawal of all Soviet troops from the country and in the revision of Party statutes to underscore Romanian nationalism. Thus, all references to the Soviet Union have been dropped, and "love for the fatherland" has taken precedence over "proletarian internationalism." To demonstrate its impartiality, but in a way deliberately calculated to annoy the Russians, Romania requires that all diplomats, Western and Soviet alike, obtain official approval for all appointments with Romanian officials and citizens. Travel restrictions are placed on American and Soviet diplomats in Bucharest in response to similar limitations placed on Romanian personnel in Washington and Moscow.

Romanization has assumed various forms, several of them treated by Professor Burks in his paper. One further example may be noted: the doubling of Party membership in the past five years. The purpose of Romanization is the creation of a mass Party, which will be both representative of all social classes and nationalist in loyalty. The Ninth Party Congress in July, 1965 abolished the candidature stage and relaxed Party disciplinary measures. At the same time, it introduced organizational changes aimed at concentrating power in the Presidium and Executive Committee of the Central Committee.

Most Communist elites are not completely secure in power and seek popular acceptance of their political legitimacy. Not unreasonably, they believe that with the passage of time their position will find increased acceptance among their people, who know since 1956 that "liberation" from outside is not feasible in a nuclear age and that evolution from within offers a better prospect for the development of a less authoritarian environment, or at least for a better material standard of living. There is, however, no necessary correlation between a lessening of authoritarian controls and an improvement in economic well-being. In East Germany, the economy and standard of living have shown improvement in recent years, but Ulbricht's dictatorship remains harsh. The creation of the Soviet Union, the East German regime, is the least secure in Eastern Europe, and depends upon the twenty Soviet divisions stationed there for its stability.

In Poland, we are witnessing a phenomenon which reverses the pattern generally found in the area: the tightening of political controls, and the deterioration of economic and material conditions. Wladyslaw Gomulka, incarcerated in 1949 on orders from Moscow, was swept to power in October, 1956 on a wave of national fervor. In momentary but momentous concert with Catholic Cardinal Wyszynski, Gomulka outfaced Khrushchev and members of the Soviet Presidium who had flown to Warsaw, and won for Poland the right to find its own road to socialism. For a few years, Poland's destalinization became a model for other East European countries: agriculture was decollectivized, Party controls were relaxed, intellectual ferment and cultural creativity roused the youth from its political apathy and torpor, the economy began to revive, and hope spread through the country. But since 1959, the intoxicating gains of the 1956-1958 period have evaporated steadily. Gomulka proved unequal to the challenge of economic reform, and sought to return to collectivization and destroy the autonomy of the Workers Councils. Alarmed at the apathy of the youth and its lack of interest in Marxism, he undertook to weaken the continuing hold of the Church in this most Catholic country in Eastern Europe. Fearful of the consequences of political liberalization, convinced that firm ties with the Soviet Union are Poland's principal guarantees against the danger of a revived Germany, and essentially unsympathetic with those who would make Poland's socialism more social-democratic than Communist, Gomulka is a man overtaken by events. A courageous symbol of opposition to Stalinism in 1956, he has since shown himself more Communist than socialist, more authoritarian than liberal, and more a political manipulator than an economic reformer, and he is respected for his defense of Poland's interests and no rivals threaten his hold on the Party.

The Yugoslav leadership has, in general, been the most cohesive in Eastern Europe, though there have been notable exceptions (i.e., Djilas and Ranković) and though there are indications that political rivalries may erupt as a consequence of the most extensive program of economic reform adopted anywhere in the Communist world. However, concern over Party legitimacy was not an inhibition to reform, because the League of Yugoslav Communists enjoys a broad base of popular support, both because of its wartime opposition to the Axis invaders and because of its genuine efforts to liberalize Yugoslav society.

POLICIES IN ACTION

Political considerations generate pressures for economic reforms, which in turn have consequences for the political system and for the exercise of power within it. The quest for popular support, the nationalistic desire to modernize and to build socialism, the search for effective levers to pry ever-greater measures of autonomy from the Soviet Union, and the stark need to compete commercially in demanding international markets have all, in varying degrees, impelled the East European leaders to embark on programs of economic reform. The realization that economic reforms are requisite for political stability has helped weaken the doctrinaire approach of many Communist leaders and has helped make them more pragmatic. But striking differences in outlook persist. Kadar assumes that material well-being and economic improvement will strengthen his policy of national reconciliation and Magyarization of the Hungarian Communist Party elite. On the other hand, Novotný of Czechoslovakia and Zhivkov of Bulgaria, both long-time, pro-Moscow, Party *apparatchiks,* fear reform will weaken their control, and therefore dole out changes sporadically and with reluctance. Ceausescu presses for modernization, but uses a model for development which most closely approximates the Soviet experience and fetters rather than frees the economy from Party constraints. Only in Yugoslavia has the leadership embraced economic reform with verve and a conscious commitment to political liberalization.

YUGOSLAVIA'S OPENING SOCIETY

In July, 1965, Yugoslavia introduced extensive economic reforms reorganizing the system of prices and production in order to make Yugoslav goods competitive in Western markets. To implement the reforms, the government also introduced further decentralization of economic and social welfare decisions. Federal subsidies and spending have been drastically reduced; a new system of commercial banks has been established and given major responsibility for the allocation of investment capital; and supply and demand play a growing role. Yugoslavia is shifting toward a quasi-market economy which will allow the optimum free flow of goods, capital, and services, within and out of the country. There is actually less central planning and control over the economy in Yugoslavia than in the United States.

Concomitant with the latest economic reforms, the Yugoslav leadership has moved determinedly to democratize the Communist Party and to lessen its manipulative and administrative functions. It seeks to guide ideologically, not to rule politically. Whether this is feasible in practice is debatable, but the Yugoslav Communists have set out to dismantle much of the Party's machinery of centralized control.

The Eighth Party Congress in December, 1964, decided to democratize itself, first, by weeding out favoritism, unhealthy ambition, and the monopolistic control of local bosses and vested bureaucratic interests and, second, by introducing the rotation system and the principle of limited re-election. Rotation means that no individual or group of individuals is permitted to secure a stranglehold on a key position or institution and that a "normal reconstitution of executive bodies" will enforce diffusion of authority. With that twist of irony for which history is noted, it was the new deposed Ranković who said: "We must continue to crush the erroneous bureaucratic belief that the worth of Communists and public officials is to be measured in terms of the number of offices they hold in government service and social organizations." In 1964, rotation was intended to apply primarily to government posts, but in 1967, the leadership accepted the necessity of applying its principles equally to the Party.

An even more ruthless reorganization of the Party was pressed in late 1966 and 1967. The leadership apparently was convinced that "the statist-bureaucratic forces" (i.e., the entrenched, old-style Communist bosses who believe and behave on the assumption that the Party should exercise control over all sectors of society) must be curbed if self-management and the economic reforms are to take root and accelerate the modernization and integration of the country. According to Mijalko Todorović, the Secretary of the newly established Executive Committee of the League of Yugoslav Communists and a person of growing importance:

> We are not dealing here with any ephemeral and temporary reorganization, but with qualitative changes in the concept of the place and role, the organization and mode of activity, with the ability of the League of Communists to transform itself, so as to ensure its constant development in the future and 'adjustment' to changes in society— changes that it itself initiates and guides—and thus to confirm, again and again, that it is the ideological-political vanguard of the working class. And finally, what we are also dealing with is the liquidation of a

dogmatic attitude towards the Communist Party and within the Communist Party.

The reorganization has two purposes: first, to transform the Party into a more open, self-critical, responsive, technically competent institution; and second, to divest top Party officials of their posts in government and in the executive organs of socio-economic institutions. Persuasion and example are to supplant the hitherto prevailing *modus operandi* of command and manipulation. The reorganization of the Party currently underway is the most far-reaching attempt to democratize a Communist Party apparatus ever tried by a Communist elite in power. Tito's hastily arranged visit to the Soviet Union in January, 1967, revealed growing Soviet disquiet over the pace and unforeseen consequences of what is occurring in Yugoslavia. Nowhere in Eastern Europe is a Communist system experimenting with so sweeping a range of daring and liberalizing innovation, and nowhere do political liberalization and economic reform mesh, interact, and generate such promising currents of change. The Soviet leaders clearly fear that the Yugoslav experiment will influence other Communist countries and make the Soviet position in Eastern Europe even more difficult.

In recent years, there have been periodic reversals and reimpositions of Party authority, but the trend has definitely been toward an ever-broadening sphere of relaxation. Intriguing indeed are the attempts to encourage citizen responsibility and participation in local affairs, to strengthen constitutional guarantees for the individual against the state, and to minimize Party interference in society. Yugoslavia is the only Communist country where a foreign visitor can enjoy unregulated travel, extensive contact with citizens from different walks of life, and open discussion of controversial subjects. Yugoslav society has a tolerance of dissent in art, literature, and even many matters of public policy, a freedom to emigrate, a receptivity to Western ideas and writings, and a relaxed attitude toward its own people that is unknown anywhere in Eastern Europe. The sentencing of Mihajlov should not be accorded disproportionate attention, and this curious harsh act in its exceptional character almost proves the rule of change within Yugoslavia. In short, Yugoslavia is groping its way toward increasingly non-authoritarian solutions to its complex problems: the success of the economic reforms and of Party reorganization will significantly influence the evolution of the political system.

Reform and Controlled Change

The countries of Eastern Europe are searching for ways to change their economic institutions and practices without jeopardizing the Party's monopoly on political power. They view Yugoslav developments with mingled skepticism and alarm. Having obtained a tolerable surcease from Soviet control over their own societies, the Eastern European leaders no longer look with uncritical admiration and envy at the phenomenon of "Titoism." On the contrary, they see its present manifestations as disruptive and dangerous.

HUNGARY

In Hungary, Janos Kadar pursues his policy of national reconciliation and reform, notwithstanding temporary economic setbacks. Though he came to power under the worst possible circumstances, installed by the Soviet Union after its brutal suppression of the 1956 revolution, he has gained a grudging measure of respect and acceptance for his pragmatism, emphasis on improving living standards, and political permissiveness. Following from his statement that "who is not against us, is with us," Kadar has made merit and not only membership in the Party the basis for promotion and reward. A general amnesty in 1963 climaxed the regime's willingness to forgive past opposition in the hope of inducing future cooperation. Police terror has diminished, tourism is actively encouraged, the arts have been revived, and cultural life is beginning to demonstrate some of its former vitality.

POLAND

Kadar launched his program of reform in 1961 with Poland, not Yugoslavia, as his model. But whereas in Hungary the tragedy of revolution and a second Soviet occupation have been mitigated by time and steady but modest liberalization, in Poland the promise of 1956 has not been realized. For a brief period liberalization was in ascendancy: Party repressiveness eased; most collective farms were dissolved; intellectual and artistic experimentation made Warsaw the *avant-garde* cultural center of Eastern Europe; and coexistence between the Catholic Church and the Communist Party seemed possible.

However, mounting economic difficulties, mismanagement, corruption, and the pervasive apathy toward politics among the youth impelled the Party leadership, which is increasingly dominated by conservative, centralist factions, to tighten labor discipline and governmental regulation of society. The ineffectiveness of reform is as much a result of the ceaseless struggle for power within the Polish Communist Party between the Stalinist and liberal factions as it is of low labor productivity and rising costs, of a shortage of capital and petty but widespread economic corruption, of rising competition in foreign markets, and of the inability of Polish agriculture to feed the Polish population. A lack of political consensus at the center is crippling the regime's capacity to deal forthrightly with pressing economic and social questions. In addition, Gomulka, concerned over the persisting prestige of the Catholic Church, even among the youth, seems to accord a higher priority to this issue than to stimulating efficiency in management and production. Unlike Hungary, which on the surface at least appears to have minimized social tensions and reached a *modus vivendi* with the Church, in Poland these factors exacerbate the political environment and preclude a concerted assault on economic problems.

CZECHOSLOVAKIA

The incredible deterioration of the Czechoslovak economy is testament to the corrosive effects of the Stalinist model of economic organization on a highly industrialized country. At the end of World War II, Czechoslovakia had a flourishing industrial establishment. The Communist coup in 1948, brought with it overcentralization, excessive planning, bureaucratic rigidity, faulty investment in low-yield projects, managerial corruption, and a sharp drop in the efficiency of Czech labor. The record of the Communist leadership in Czechoslovakia, at least economically, is the worst in Western Europe.

Prague introduced its long-heralded, oft-delayed economic reform on January 1, 1967, but with proverbial Czech caution. Although the "Sik Plan" (named after Professor Ota Sik) originally stressed the need for rapid restructuring of the pricing system, the fear and enmity of the entrenched, old-guard Czechoslovak political leaders has resulted in a policy of creeping gradualism, without significant political liberalization, which could mire the economy more deeply in the morass of what the French once termed *immobilisme*. A parallel situation exists in Bulgaria.

Czechoslovakia's Antonín Novotný and Todor Zhivkov, his Bulgarian counterpart, dominate the Communist Party machines in their respective countries. Both are Stalinists who have survived by cunning, mastery of political organization and in-fighting, service to Moscow, and occasional lip service to destalinization. Their concern is with power not progress. Rigid in outlook, suspicious of liberalization in any sector, and skeptical of the predictions of their economists, they fear that economic reform will bring in its wake political reverberations, and accordingly have suppressed the reformers whenever possible. For example, in 1962 Novotný had Rudolf Barak, then Vice-Premier and member of the Politburo, imprisoned on trumped up charges for trying to organize a reformist anti-Stalinist faction within the Party. In 1963, he removed from office Premier Viliam Siroky and Karol Bacilek, a Presidium member, in a maneuver that eliminated from the scene two comrades of long-standing. Though themselves Slovak, they were under attack for their role in the liquidation of Slovak leaders during the Stalin period. Their elimination by Novotný was engineered to strengthen the Czech faction at the expense of the Slovak minority, which tended to be the center of anti-Novotný sentiment, and simultaneously to deflect Soviet pressures for destalinization by purging several Stalinists, while leaving his own clique untouched.

BULGARIA

If Bulgaria's economic stagnation has been less dramatic, it is nevertheless at a much lower level of economic development. Zhivkov and the provincial Party oligarchs are conservative and authoritarian. The system they have fashioned may be described as Stalinism without terror; or as cautious decompression, if one has hopes for the experimental, limited economic changes that were introduced in 1966. Bulgaria's limited industrialization has been due largely to Soviet assistance. Criticism is not tolerated, and a generation is coming of age that is politically apathetic and economically unmotivated. Conformity is prized above creativity, and wages are controlled and low. Geographical isolation from the mainstream of European cultural and intellectual currents serves somewhat to mitigate the leadership's anxiety over the influx of foreign tourists, who are becoming a major source of sorely needed hard currency. From Sofia, even Prague seems in ferment.

ROMANIA

In neighboring Romania, "desovietization" sparked extraordinary economic development. The emphasis is on industrial expansion and modernization; the model is Stalinist, with priority accorded to heavy industry, collectivization and tight labor discipline. However, unlike the Soviet Union, Romania is encouraging foreign private investment, and France, West Germany, and Italy have already negotiated sizeable projects.

"Desovietization" has not meant internal democratization. Romania remains a highly centralized, closely regulated police state, which helps explain the Party's recent concern that the imbalance of the boom may require of it a measure of administrative liberalization. At a meeting of the Central Committee on December 23, 1966, Ceausescu presented a bill of short-comings: a low level of diversification of the machine-building industry; technological backwardness; high cost, low-quality goods; poorly coordinated planning; and a need "to combat megalomania and trends toward gigantomania." His report warned the Party not to take refuge in the impressive growth rate but to face the deficiencies:

> We may speak about the economic superiority of socialism over capitalism, but as long as certain advanced capitalist countries produce cheaper and at a higher technical level, we shall not be able to prove this superiority.

Ceausescu directed attention to the importance of international trade and, by implication, of Western European markets.

The suggested solutions are Soviet in tenor: the assumption by the Party of active and pervasive direction "of the whole national economy, of every sector, be it state, cooperative or private"; and the imposition of stringent labor discipline, with severe penalties for low productivity and excessive absenteeism. In their approach to internal development, Romanian leaders are close to the narrow, authoritarian outlook of their Communist counterparts in East Germany and Poland. They are not attracted by the Yugoslav or Hungarian experience, possibly because they feel more secure and familiar with the centralist and Stalinist mode of effectuating, yet controlling change.

Everywhere economic difficulties have forced the leaders to listen to the reformers, but they are hesitant, in varying degrees, to loosen the reins of Party controls. They fear relaxation might generate demands which could be curbed only by repression, a counter-productive response of last resort, and also make more difficult harnessing national energies for the task of industrialization and modernization. Clearly, a reliable recipe for the "Goulash Communism"

Khrushchev commended during a visit to Hungary several years ago continues to elude the leaders of Eastern Europe.

THE SUCCESSION PROBLEM

We have noted that ultimate political power in Communist societies is centered in the Party and that the decision makers within the Party are relatively few in number. There remains unanswered the question of how and by whom Party leaders are chosen. As long as the Party oligarchs take precedence over constitutionally elected officials, i.e., Presidents and Prime Ministers, then the transfer of power, under whatever conditions, must be presumed to take place within the institutional framework of the Party. In the struggle for power, personal rivalries beget factions, and factions ally across institutional lines in quest of strength. The more developed the society, the greater is the likelihood of ever-shifting coalitions of representatives of all major power centers, for example, the military and governmental bureaucracies. In the absence of orderly and open procedures for determining the succession, our data about the process of selection itself are limited and do not lend themselves to generalization.

The political longevity of the dominant figures has been remarkable. Ulbricht and Novotný date from the Stalin period. Zhivkov has dominated the Bulgarian scene since 1954, Gomulka, Poland, and Kadar, Hungary, since 1956. Tito, the revolutionary turned statesman, has been a symbol of national unity and politically unassailable since 1945.

Leadership crises have varied. In Romania, in March, 1965, Gheorghe Gheorghiu-Dej died and power transferred to his heir-apparent, Nicolae Ceausescu, with singular dispatch and absence of uncertainty, an event thus far unique in the postwar history of Eastern Europe. Two other crises, in Bulgaria and Yugoslavia, deserve attention, because the conditions which precipitated them may recur.

In April, 1965, a group of Bulgarian Army officers tried to depose Todor Zhivkov. From all indications, the initial warning of the plot came from the Soviet security apparatus in Sofia, thus eliminating one of the ways by which Moscow "intervenes" in support of pro-Muscovite factions. Zhivkov denounced the affair as the work of a few disgruntled "adventurers and power-seekers" in the lower echelons with no popular support who sought to introduce a pro-Peiping orientation. A contrary view suggests that the men shared a common partisan background in World War II and were motivated by a desire to gain for Bulgaria a greater measure of autonomy. Such a group no doubt also exists in Poland and bears watching in the future.

On July 1, 1966, President Tito announced the resignation of Vice-President Aleksandar Ranković and his removal from all Party positions. This was the first breach in the Yugoslav Communist hierarchy since the Djilas affair of 1954; more significantly, it was the first crisis in the maneuvering for position among the would-be heirs-apparent to Tito. Ranković had worked under Tito for more than three decades and was generally regarded as his most likely successor. Using his enormous power to build up a personal following in the secret police and in the Serbian Communist Party, he apparently tried to sabotage the economic reforms and hinder efforts to democratize Party practices and personnel policy. Tito knew of these "deformations" as early as 1962, but was galvanized to action only after learning that Ranković men had placed listening devices in Tito's own residences.

It is as difficult to generalize about the succession problem on the basis of episodic events as it is to evaluate the relative strengths of the men waiting for their opportunities to seize power. In Eastern Europe, as in the Soviet Union, the outcome of political struggle is determined in Party cabals, whose inner workings are shrouded in the secrecy and isolation that typify all Communist leaderships. Although we do not know how "elections" or transfers of power are managed, we do know that each "election" and each salient thrust for power has differed somewhat from the previous one and has affected, and in turn been affected by, the evolving political system in which it occurs.

Constitutionalism and Governmental Processes

East European reformers are coming to perceive the integral relationship between the realization of economic goals and the revitalization of the governmental and administrative structures through which the economy is managed. The excessively centralized and detailed Party supervision over all aspects of economic and political life that prevailed during the period of postwar political consolidation and institutional upheaval placed impossible burdens on the Party. It bred swollen, unresponsive bureaucracies, managerial ineptness, and indifference among the masses. Above all, it

vitiated the potential of governmental institutions for responsible
participation in the administration of the economy and, indeed, of
all non-political functions. Realizing that show-piece constitutions
and rubber-stamp legislatures served only to widen the gap between
the Party and the people, and that the strengthening of economic
structures demands a more rational and flexible utilization of all
political instrumentalities, Party leaderships have set out to invest
governmental institutions with an importance and vitality hitherto
lacking. Each country in Eastern Europe is grappling with the problem of how to vest some authority in governmental institutions so as
to make them more efficient transmission belts of Party policies and
more responsible administrative agencies for the implementation of
economic objectives without, however, weakening the overall political role of the Party. To date, bold strides have been taken only in
Yugoslavia, though the half-hearted innovations elsewhere in Eastern
Europe are also not without interest or long-term significance.

YUGOSLAV INNOVATIONS

On April 7, 1963, Yugoslavia adopted a new constitution intended
to establish a more viable governmental system. It provided for a
diminution in the Party's interference in the management of the
economy; it strengthened local self-government; and it introduced
more effective checks on the power of the federal government, in
particular on the Federal Executive Council (the highest executive
body of government) to make it more responsive to the legislature
which has, concomitantly, been upgraded in influence. Developments of the past few years have invested the federal branches of
government with an autonomous authority that has exceeded the
original mandate of the framers of the constitution and lent support
to the view that the Yugoslavs are genuinely interested in fashion-
ing governmental institutions that will have important functions in
the country's move toward social democracy.

Under the constitution, Yugoslavia established one of the most
complex legislative systems in the world. The national legislature,
known as the Federal Assembly, consists of five Chambers: the Federal Chamber, the Economic Chamber, the Chamber of Education
and Culture, the Chamber of Social Welfare and Health, and the
Political-Organizational Chamber. Though all are nominally co-
equal, the Federal Chamber, or upper house, is the most important
because it elects the members of the Federal Executive Council, plays
a role in the formulation of policy pertaining to foreign relations,

national defense, and general internal security affairs, and appoints the members of the Constitutional Court. Each Chamber has 120 deputies, except the Federal Chamber, which has 190 deputies, 70 of whom are designated as the members of the Chamber of Nationalities by the six republican assemblies and by the two autonomous provinces of Vojvodina and Kosovo-Metohija. The Chamber of Nationalities is convened separately only when an issue involving the nationalities or a proposal to amend the constitution is on the agenda. At all other times, the deputies designated for this Chamber are constituted as part of the Federal Chamber.

The Party sought to ensure its preeminent position by limiting the power of the legislature through diffusion of authority and limitation on terms in office. By having the members of the five Chambers elected from the functional institutions of society, i.e. trade unions, workers' councils, and educational institutions, the Party envisaged a situation in which the deputies would tend to be technocrats rather than politicians and the expertise of the specialist would be brought to bear on concrete problems in the respective Chambers. In addition, by limiting the tenure of a deputy in the Federal Assembly to two four-year terms, it hoped to engender among professionally competent but politically unambitious individuals a concept of public service unknown in the Balkans. Four years are, admittedly, not sufficient to make any definitive statements about the viability of the new Yugoslav governmental institutions, but they provide a basis for tentative evaluation.

Since 1963, the Federal Assembly has introduced a number of modifications of its procedures and committee structure designed to enhance its role in shaping legislation and in restraining the powers of the executive and administrative bodies of government. A brief look at the functioning of one of the Chambers, the Economic Chamber, and its relationship to the Federal Chamber may contribute to our understanding of the Yugoslav legislative system in general.

The Economic Chamber is responsible, along with the Federal Chamber, for discussing and approving all economic and financial legislation. Unlike the deputies of the Federal Chamber, who are professionally involved in political affairs, the members of the Economic Chamber are specialists and technicians in their area of competence. These men perform an act of public service by serving in the Chamber at the same time that they continue their professional work in the enterprises, institutes, and universities with which they are affiliated. About 25 to 30 percent of their working time is absorbed by governmental service.

The Economic Chamber has two kinds of committees: the Council (*Odbor*), which is the more important, and the Commission (*Komisija*). Although not officially institutionalized, the Councils and Commissions have, in fact, been functioning as permanently constituted bodies. The day-by-day, substantive work of the Economic Chamber is carried on by its various Councils, each of which is responsible for a functional area, e.g. manufacturing, agriculture, or commerce. The Commissions tend to deal with non-substantive matters.

At the end of 1965, the Federal Assembly established a new institution, the Parliamentary Commission, in order to cope with a *de facto* political difficulty which had arisen between the Federal Executive Council and the Federal Assembly. Under the Yugoslav governmental system, the principal initiative for new legislation comes from the FEC, which is the organ of the Federal Assembly entrusted with political-executive functions, among which the introduction of bills and legislative proposals is particularly important. Members of the FEC are not, however, heads of individual ministries of the government, as in a true parliamentary system. The President of the FEC functions as the Prime Minister. In a sense, the FEC and the President of the Federation (Tito) constitute the executive branch of government.

In the summer of 1965, the Federal Secretariat for Foreign Trade drafted proposed legislation which the FEC, after appropriate debate and modification, submitted for approval to the Federal Assembly. The President of the Assembly then sent the proposed legislation to the Federal Chamber and the Economic Chamber for review and approval. Both Chambers disagreed with the proposals and rejected them, returning them to FEC. An unforeseen situation thus developed in which the Federal Assembly found itself at variance with the Federal Executive Council which, though part of the Assembly, found itself thwarted by that body. What emerged was a disagreement between two centers of power and a polarization of views in the Assembly that had not been foreseen by the constitution-makers. To avoid a recurrence of such disputes (which did not arise out of any clash of political or ideological positions, but from differences among specialists on foreign trade), the Parliamentary Commissions were established.

There are eight Parliamentary Commissions which deal *inter alia* with issues of price-formation, social planning, the banking system, foreign trade, and health services. Established as *ad hoc* bodies, they are convened only in response to particular problems. Each Commission includes deputies, members of the FEC, officials from government ministries, and experts brought in from the academic and scientific community for assistance on specific problems. It is designed to include all shades of opinion and to make recommendations on the basic principles for the drafting of specific legislation. The Parliamentary Commissions are not intended to cancel or circumvent the normal functioning of the Councils and Commissions of the various Chambers of the Federal Assembly. Rather, they are to facilitate agreement on the basic principles of proposed legislation, after which the Chambers will be free to disagree with and to modify such specific provisions as they consider necessary. It is hoped that the Parliamentary Commissions will provide a vehicle for reconciling the thinking of the officials in the governmental ministries, the FEC, and the Federal Assembly, the assumption being that once agreement on principles has been reached in the Commissions, the task of gaining approval for legislation will be accomplished with minimum discord.

Yugoslav officials stress two points in discussing the future of the Federal Assembly. First, procedural innovations are certain to continue, as the Assembly tries to function more efficiently and to avoid jurisdictional disputes. Second, the Assembly is an active and constructive legislative body, and not one established "to engage in hand gymnastics." It functions as a corrective to the Federal Executive Council, whose activities have received systematic and public criticism and scrutiny. Officials acknowledge that the classical division of executive and legislative power does not exist in the Yugoslav system, but contend that it would be a mistake therefore to conclude that the Federal Assembly is a bogus institution dominated by the FEC and that it does not have an important role to play in the evolution of a more democratic system.

Another major institutional innovation is the Constitutional Court. Created in 1963, this eleven-man Court is charged with responsibility for curbing arbitrary and unconstitutional behavior by administrative and government officials, for protecting the basic rights and freedoms of the individual against unwarranted "bureaucratic" exercises of power, and for adjudicating disputes among the political and socio-economic institutions of society. As a watchdog against arbitrary governmental practices, the Court has already made notable contributions toward defining and preserving "constitutionality and legality." A measure of its impact on the political system is in the increasing attention which administrators and legislators accord to Court decisions and to its probable attitude on a range of problems. In no other Communist country has a judicial body been given so broad a range of independent powers *vis-a-vis* other governmental bodies or such latitude to intrude into legislative matters that, in the opinion of the Court, are affected with a legal or constitutional character.

THE HIATUS IN GOVERNMENTAL REFORM

The hesitation of Communist Parties in Eastern Europe to experiment with liberalization of governmental processes and structures is a reminder that political evolution there will almost certainly remain slow. Though there have been changes, they have clearly not wrought any basic alteration in power relationships nor given the electorate significant opportunity for expressing preferences. A number of innovations may be mentioned, with the caution that these are limited in scope and isolated in implementation.

Communist governments in Poland, Czechoslovakia, Hungary, and Romania on occasion permit more than one Party-approved candidate to run for office in a few constituencies, thereby affording the electorate an opportunity to reject unpopular candidates. However, the nominations are controlled by the Party, and the number of electoral districts in which more than one candidate is offered on the ballot is limited. For example, out of the 349 seats filled in the 1967 parliamentary elections in Hungary, only nine were filled by deputies from constituencies with two candidates; at the local level, the number of "contested" seats was greater, but still less than one per cent of the total number of offices filled. Comparable data for the other countries are even less impressive.

Some leaders in Eastern Europe have talked of rejuvenating the Parliaments and of assigning the national legislatures more active and meaningful functions in shaping legislation, but few actions have been taken. For example, the Poles made attempts (since arrested) to give the Sejm limited powers to review and criticize proposed legislation, initiate bills, and question Cabinet Ministers on their areas of responsibility. Administrative reorganization of local government in Czechoslovakia and Hungary appears to have eased the Party's propensity toward managerial interference. The composition of the executive bodies of government is determined in Party enclaves and not in Parliament. The legislatures do not legislate; they meet for short periods and discuss rather than deliberate, for power lies elsewhere and the deputies know this.

The weaknesses of parliament are known by the population and the Party leaders do not even pretend that they seek to encourage the formation of formal opposition groups in Parliament. However, they persist in retaining the *form* of coalition government, that is to say, governments organized either in broadly-based, mass coalitions of all acceptable hues of socialist affiliation (e.g. the People's Patriotic Front in Hungary) or along multi-Party lines in which the Communist Party has a majority of seats and the ultimate political authority. Thus, in Poland, besides the Polish United Workers (Communist) Party, there are four parties which have more than one-third of the seats. Retention by Communist leaders of these decorative coalitions connotes the persistence among the general population of pre-war Party loyalties and appeals, as well as the absence of overwhelming popular commitment to Communist parties.

The unwillingness of Party leaders to enact meaningful reforms of governmental institutions reflects their ingrained resistance to relinquishing any power, however marginal. At the same time, this failure limits their ability to generate the deeper sense of public responsibility and participation upon which the prospects of economic rejuvenation heavily depend. The Party has traditionally regarded governmental institutions as instrumentalities for carrying out the administration of the economy. To promote the more effective functioning of administrative agencies, it may have to infuse governmental institutions with a credible vitality, lest indifference continue to pervade the political atmosphere at every level of society. The reluctant oligarchs of Eastern Europe have only begun to comprehend the nature of this dilemma.

SOME OBSERVATIONS

Even a cursory retrospective review of former assumptions concerning Eastern Europe highlights the impermanence of conventional political wisdom, the distortions inherent in political perceptions, and the ambiguity and complexity of political relationships in an ever-changing world. We need careful, continuing, critical re-evaluations of goals and capabilities, both of our allies and of our opponents. There is no fixed lodestar in the constellation of evolving political systems. Nations are seldom static, and what they appear to be may no longer accurately reflect the reality of what they are or where they are heading.

Eastern Europe has changed enormously in the past decade and will continue to evolve dramatically in the years ahead. The forces and trends set loose since Stalin are far from running their course: East European nationalism, the pressures for internal liberalization and modernization, the cacophony of a differentiated Communist camp, the evolutionary pressures of Soviet domestic developments, and the interest in Western technology and culture are all catalytic agents.

Eastern Europe's changed relationship with the Soviet Union is the most notable development of the post-Stalin period. Each country has claimed for itself a measure of national autonomy which reflects the intensity of nationalist feelings and the skill of the respective Communist leaderships in inducing a lessening of Soviet control. While Moscow seems prepared to accept some national autonomy in Eastern Europe, provided the political configuration remains Communist in character, it is seeking new ways to assure at least a level of cohesion consonant with what it considers essential for Soviet security.

The East European countries have accepted the need for economic reform, but seek to limit its liberalizing effects on the political system. The Yugoslav experience shows that reform, if it is to be successful, cannot be confined to one area, but requires political and social liberalization. If the liberalization "virus" cannot be fought indefinitely by the confining political "antibodies," then the transformation of East European societies may become more pronounced, especially with the emergence to power of a generation not steeped in ideological dogma, emotional attachments to the Soviet Union, or fear of its own people. The form and style of each political system will no doubt reflect the country's historical and cultural distinctiveness, which, in turn, had helped to shape the particular character of the Communist regime.

Internal liberalization is inevitable because no developed political system can long progress if it insists on maintaining a stultifying atmosphere that cows its citizenry and discourages initiative. But liberalization is not synonymous with democratization. While the lot of the individual has improved, his capacity to affect the choice of leaders has not. Political power remains oligarchical and largely immune to the wishes or pressures of the masses, though these may be manipulated by one or another faction seeking control. It is presumptuous to regard democratization as a commodity which can be exported. On the other hand, liberalization is more susceptible to the inputs of outsiders.

Inter-cultural penetration and intensified interaction with the West can contribute to the internal liberalization of everyday life in these countries. The process is circuitous but can be illustrated. Thus, the desire for expanded trade with the West, which is motivated by the quest for modernization and greater independence, requires that East European leaders fashion an internal environment which will stimulate efficiency and production of quality goods capable of competing in Western markets.

Finally, nationalism is not an unmixed blessing. Eastern Europe has in the past suffered from the pretentions and divisive consequences of exaggerated nationalism. Thus, we see that notwithstanding Yugoslavia's remarkable record since 1951, its viability as a nation-state still depends on the ability of the Serbs and Croats to transcend historic animosities and mini-visions of emotional but dubious grandeur. However welcome the manifestations of East European autonomy within the Soviet camp, they should not be regarded as ends in themselves. In "building-bridges" to Eastern Europe, the West should strive for liberalization *and* stability. This entails a sympathetic understanding of legitimate Soviet security and economic interests in the area. Friendly relations between Eastern Europe and the Soviet Union need not be incompatible with Western objectives of a stable Eastern Europe of liberalizing societies which is also participating in the creation of a new Europe. The West should not expect Eastern Europe to divest itself completely of all Soviet influence. Geography, shared ideological goals, and the realities of international power preclude such a situation. To paraphrase what the Mexican dictator, Porfirio Diaz, once said of Mexico and the United States: "Poor Eastern Europe, so far from God—so close to the Soviet Union." Bridge-building can succeed only if there is cooperation and understanding on all sides.

Nicolas Spulber

3

Economic Modernization

For the economist, modern economic growth is "an application of the industrial system, i.e., a system of production based on increasing use of scientific knowledge." It implies high rates of growth in total and per capita product; a sharp increase in both output capacity and in efficiency; a rise in the relative shares of manufacture and public utilities and a decrease in the share of agriculture in total product; changes in the pattern of final demand and in import-export opportunities; and diversification of a population's skills and an increase in its mobility.

The political scientist and the sociologist have pointed out that the corollaries of these changes are "social mobilization" and various processes of "structural differentiation." The first term refers to the erosion of major clusters of old social, economic, and psychological commitments, and to the processes conditioned by exposure to the various aspects of modern life through changes in occupation, in residence, in urbanization, and in the spread of literacy and of mass media. Structural differentiation, on the other hand, is equated with major changes in the social structure characterized by the development of "specialized and diversified types of social organization," "wide non-traditional 'national' or even supernational group identifications," and "wide regulative and allocative mechanisms and organization in all major institutional spheres."

Author of a number of books on the economics of Eastern Europe and the U.S.S.R., Nicolas Spulber *is professor of economics at Indiana University.*

This paper focuses on the narrower aspects of economic growth as they are defined by the economist. The complex corollaries of economic growth are not ignored, but they are noted only to the extent that they blend directly with specific economic processes.

Patterns of Industrialization

The effort to introduce modern economic growth into Eastern Europe long preceded the Communist regimes, which have continued and changed the direction and intensity of the earlier programs. Economic growth has attained different intensities and exercised different impacts in the highly industrialized countries of the area, such as Czechoslovakia; in the primarily agricultural countries with significant industrial facilities, such as Poland and Hungary; and in the less developed countries, such as Romania, Bulgaria, Yugoslavia and Albania. The main economic goal of the primarily agricultural countries has not substantively changed since before the war; it may be summarized as "rapid industrialization." The main economic goals of the highly developed countries of the area have been, on the other hand, qualitatively different. Since 1945, these goals have basically been those of restructuring and re-equipping and then of expanding an already substantial industrial establishment.

POLISH PROGRAM BEFORE WORLD WAR II

The most significant effort before World War II toward formulating a strategy of development, devising an integrated scheme of development, and taking decisive steps for modernizing the economy was made by Poland. Begun in 1936 and ended by the Nazi invasion in 1939, the Polish scheme of comprehensive industrialization focused upon the development of a basic region, the so-called Industrial Central District located in the Warsaw-Cracow-Lwow triangle in order to achieve economies of scale. It encompassed between one-sixth and one-seventh of the area and population of the country, a region with 5,500,000 people. The region, the most poverty-stricken of Poland, was selected because it was a central location best suited for defense industries, key raw materials sources were nearby, large surpluses of peasant labor were available, and it had a good natural transportation axis, the Vistula.

The first three years of the program were the beginning of a grandiose industrialization scheme to be implemented over a fifteen-year period, extending from 1939 to 1954, and intended to change the occupational structure of the country's manpower from 70:30 (the ratio of agricultural to nonagricultural manpower) to 50:50. In order to launch this program, the Polish government increased sharply the mobilization of domestic investable resources, expanded its foreign indebtedness, invested directly in the region, and attracted a large inflow of private investment with a variety of tax exemptions, credits, and grants. During the three years of actual plan implementation, the industrial enterprises completed in the area absorbed 90,000 gainfully employed, compared to a total of 800,000 then employed in all Polish industries.

HUNGARY

In March 1938, Hungary announced a Five-Year Plan intended to expand rapidly both defense capabilities and productive capacity. Over five years, three-fifths of a total investment of one billion pengoes ($290 million at the official, and $190 million at the actual exchange rate) were to be channeled toward industry and armament production, one-fifth toward transport and communications, and one-fifth toward agriculture. No detailed plan was worked out, and full coordination of the government's economic activities did not begin until 1940. However, due partly to increases in both territory and population from Romania and then to war mobilization, the investment target was reached earlier. By 1940, two-thirds of the volume of investment had already been collected; by 1944, when the war reached Hungarian territory, the effects of substantial government spending were clearly visible. Industrial capacity and output had expanded appreciably. In the five years between 1938 and 1943, Hungary's industrial manpower had risen by over 100,000, while during the preceding fifteen years the industrial labor increment had been only 90,000.

ROMANIA

Romania also attempted the formulation of a comprehensive development program in the late 1930's, integrating policies concerning industrial location, industrial concentration, raw materials, "nationalization of capital," labor, output, prices, and consumption. A detailed official study fixing "criteria of behavior for the formulation of an economic plan" was published by a "Supreme Economic Council" in 1939. However, planning efforts had to be interrupted, the country was soon forced to cede a large part of its territory and population to Hungary, and it then became fully involved in World War II.

In Romania, as in all the other less-developed countries of the area except Albania, both before and after World War II, state involvement in the economy tended to concentrate upon three lines: direct investment in heavy industries closely connected with defense; direct or indirect participation in the provision of developmental infrastructure, transport, power, public utilities, and education; and provision of a variety of stimuli, such as protective tariffs, tax inducements, grants, and credits, to domestic or foreign private entrepreneurs for the development of industries. State involvement grew more extensive in scope and complexity as minimal developmental requirements were met and as new pressure groups of industrialists, bankers, landowners, workers, and peasants began to unite and compete for assistance.

THE POSTWAR PATTERN

After World War II and the assumption of power by the Communists, strategies of development and a set of instruments to carry them out identical to those in the Soviet "model" were adopted by each of the East European countries. Each country decided to reproduce in miniature the Soviet economy, and to emphasize investment in both capital goods and human resources. Each country allocated its investable resources in such a way as to speed the growth of industry relative to growth of agriculture and services; the growth of heavy industry relative to the growth of light industry; and the growth of power, metallurgy and machinery branches of heavy industry relative to the growth rates of all other branches. Moreover, a massive effort to educate, retrain, and upgrade the available industrial manpower and to absorb a large part of the surplus agricultural manpower took place throughout the area.

During a period which extended from the mid- or late 1940's to the end of the 1950's, and which might be called the "command economy" phase, centralistic methods of planning and management of the Stalinist type dominated. In each country, the central planning body, under the control of the party-state, made all major economic decisions. Except in Yugoslavia after the early 1950's, the state relied on direct controls of investment, allocation, operation, work conditions, prices, and all transactions with foreign countries. Simultaneously, the sphere of state ownership was expanded to include the "commanding heights" in each economy: all manufacturing proper, banking, transport and communications, and trade, as well as a certain part of the land, the rest being organized in all the countries except Yugoslavia and Poland into peasant collective farms.

Since the mid-1960's, a number of attempts have been made throughout the area, except perhaps in Romania, toward establishing a new set of instruments to carry out the same strategy of development. Little by little, a new phase called "new economic management" has started to emerge. However, an entirely new type of economic leadership and decision-making has taken hold only in Yugoslavia. The new system is to rely eventually mostly on indicative rather than on command planning, and on monetary and fiscal instruments, rather than on direct output and allocation orders. The goals and the main institutional framework thus remain the same; the instruments for carrying these goals out vary, however, from one regime to another.

Postwar Emphases and Results

STRATEGIES

The communist strategy of economic progress has concentrated on the development of a few leading industries, on the massive introduction of advanced technology, and on a major expansion in the scale of output and labor intake in industry as a whole. The Communists have stepped up sharply the volume and rate of investment in order to achieve great growth. They have sought extensive development of the "engineering" industries and of power, steel, and metal in order to create a firm domestic base for further industrialization, reap the benefits of external economies of scale, and achieve demand to match the expanded output.

During certain years (1949–52, 1958–62), investments rose to 20–25 per cent of the net material product and, in certain cases, to as much as even 35 per cent. However, during the periods of sharp economic and social imbalances which followed, investment decelerated in irregular and halting steps, leading even to disinvestment in certain countries. While the accelerating-decelerating pattern of investment has had seriously disequilibrating effects, the big leaps of the early fifties, late fifties, and (at least for some countries) of the mid-1960's, have had a substantial impact on productive capacity and on employment. Even in the poor years, investment has generally been above the prewar averages of 4–5 per cent of the national product. As much as 70–85 per cent of total investment has gone into industry, agriculture and transport, and the balance into education, communal construction and housing. Industry itself has received from 40–50 per cent of total investment.

SHIFTS IN COMPOSITION OF NATIONAL PRODUCT

Expansion in capacity in the leading branches has led to significant shifts in the composition of the national product. The relative share of manufacturing output has risen, while that of agriculture has contracted. The relative shares of power, ferrous and nonferrous metallurgy, and the engineering industries have risen in total manufacturing, while those of the light and food industries have decreased. According to official 1964 data, the relative shares of manufacturing in total output ranged from 40–80 per cent in Yugoslavia, Bulgaria and Romania, to 51 per cent in Poland, and 63–65 per cent in Hungary, Czechoslovakia, and East Germany. Comparing per capita income with the data on the shares of industry and agriculture in net national product, we may infer that in the mid-1960's a rise in manufacturing from 40–48 to 51 per cent and, conversely, a fall in agriculture from 28–34 per cent to 21–22 per cent, were associated in the area with a rise in per capita income of from roughly $600–$900 to $900–$1,200. In addition, we may infer that a rise in manufacturing from 51 to 63–65 per cent and, conversely, a fall in agriculture from 21–22 per cent to 10–14 per cent, were associated with a rise in per capita income of from $900–$1,200 to a range roughly from $1,300–$1,500. Three levels of development were thus apparent in the area: an upper tier, the industrialized countries, East Germany and Czechoslovakia; a lower tier, Yugoslavia, Bulgaria, Romania and, of course, Albania; and a middle tier, Poland and Hungary.

INDUSTRIAL GROWTH

During the 1950's, the relative share of machinery in total manufacturing output rose throughout the area. It grew from 9–13 to 13–24 per cent in Bulgaria and Romania; from 9–19 to 20–27 per cent in Poland and Hungary; and from 20–24 to over 33 per cent in Czechoslovakia and East Germany. The growth of capital goods outputs took place simultaneously with rapid development of both the raw materials bases and the industries processing materials previously exported in raw or semifinished states. Significant efforts were thus made to develop, on the one hand, the energy sources

Table 1: Eastern Europe and U.S.S.R. Net Material Product * by Origin, in 1964. Percentages (Underlying data at current prices).

	Agriculture	Industry	Construction	Transportation & communication	Wholesale & Retail Trade	Other
East Germany	10	65	5	5	13	2
Czechoslovakia	14	64	9	3	9	1
Hungary	21	63	10	5	—	1
Poland	22	51	9	6	10	2
Bulgaria	34	45	7	4	8	2
Romania	30	48	8	4	7	3
Yugoslavia	28	40	8	6	12	6
U.S.S.R.	21	54	9	5	11	

* Net National Product excluding services not directly connected with production.

SOURCE: United Nations, *Yearbook of National Accounts Statistics*, 1965 (New York, 1966), *passim*, especially 464-465.

(solid fuel, liquid fuel, gas and hydroelectricity), the ferrous and nonferrous metals and metallurgical coke, and a variety of other raw materials, and on the other hand, to expand machinery construction, chemicals, plastics, electronics, and even nucleonics.

The pace of growth in manufacturing output was particularly vigorous in some of the less-developed countries, notably Romania and Bulgaria, where it reached as much as 9.4 and 9.9 per cent per year over the period 1951–64. The slowest pace was registered in some of the most developed countries, particularly in Czechoslovakia, where the rate of growth decelerated appreciably in the 1960's. While the official growth claims are exaggerated, it seems nevertheless certain that over the decade 1955–64, industrial output rose by as much as nearly 150 per cent in the less-developed countries, from 80–100 per cent in the middle tier countries, and around 70 per cent in the upper, most developed tier of the area. For the area as a whole, a rate of growth of roughly 8 per cent per year throughout 1951–64 compared favorably to a rate of 6–7 per cent in Western Europe for the same period. (Table 2)

Following the deep dislocations brought about by the war and the unsettling impact of various postwar reorganization measures of the countryside, land reforms and collectivization, farm output recovered slowly. According to official data, during 1959–64 farm output rose by as much as 6.4 and 4.6 per cent per year only in Albania and Bulgaria. In the other countries, the over-all increases were only 1.4–2.2 per annum, with the livestock output increasing more rapidly than the crop output. According to Western estimates agricultural output in the early 1960's was still only around 80–90 per cent of prewar figures in Czechoslovakia and East Germany, at roughly the prewar level in Hungary, and from 10 to 30 per cent over prewar output in the other countries. These figures compare unfavorably with the vigorous growth of agricultural production in Western Europe, where growth over prewar levels ranged between 38 per cent in West Germany to over 65 per cent in Denmark.

Table 2: Eastern Europe. Indices of Industrial Production and Rates of Growth. Prewar, 1955 and 1964.

	Official estimates of gross value of output				Western estimates of industrial output *			
				1955 = 100				
	Prewar	1950	1964	Rate of growth, 1958-64	Prewar	1950	1964	Rate of growth, 1961-64
East Germany	—	52	192	7.8	80	59	166	7.7
Czechoslovakia	44	58	198	7.4	69	80	167	5.4
Hungary	—	53	203	5.0	57	65	179	7.5
Poland	—	47	219	9.1	53	63	196	8.4
Bulgaria	14	45	276	13.0	40	67	250	9.9
Romania	33	49	284	13.0	49	69	244	9.4
Yugoslavia	—	41	286	12.1	—	—	—	—

* Including construction and handicraft production.

SOURCES: Official indices from National Statistical Yearbooks. Rates of growth are based on official data from *Mir Sotsialisma v tsifrakh i faktakh 1964 god* (The Socialist World in Facts and Figures, 1964, Moscow, 1965), 114. Western data are from Maurice Ernst, "Postwar Economic Growth in Eastern Europe (A comparison with Western Europe)," in *New Directions in the Soviet Economy*, Studies prepared for the Subcommittee on Foreign Economic Policy of the Joint Economic Committee, 89th Congress, second session (Washington, 1966), 883.

Changing Manpower Supply, Composition, and Growth

Persistent effort was required to form rapidly a larger management and technical elite, to expand, restructure, and upgrade the supply of artisans and industrial manpower, to absorb into the growing producers' goods industries a vast influx of unskilled labor from the countryside, and to readjust education at a variety of levels. Appreciable shifts in urban-rural ratios, significant changes in growth rates of industrializing communities versus lagging towns, decelerating population growth rates, important shifts in manpower structure, the fall in illiteracy, and the rise in the supply of high level professional power all underline the deep changes brought about by rapid industrialization.

URBANIZATION

The process of urbanization, already well under way in the inter-war years, accelerated substantially during the 1950's and early 1960's. The ratio of urban to total population rose by the beginning of the 1960's to 28–32 per cent in the less-developed countries to 40– 48 per cent in Hungary and Poland, and remained rather stationary at the prewar level of around 48 per cent in Czechoslovakia and at 72 per cent in East Germany. The bulk of the population, at least 70 per cent, continued to live in urban or rural localities with less than 10,000 inhabitants, except in Poland, where the percentage dropped to around 60 per cent, and in Hungary and East Germany, where this percentage fluctuated around 55 per cent. Entirely new industrial towns were created and, in certain cases, small communities were enormously expanded.

EMPLOYMENT PATTERNS

Significant changes took place in employment; the shares of both manufacturing and services increased, while that of agriculture contracted. The pace of change was particularly strong in the less-developed countries. The official data for Yugoslavia, Romania, and Bulgaria indicate that the share of industry in total employment rose significantly during 1950–63. For the first two, the rise was roughly from 10–14 to 22–24 per cent, and for the latter, from roughly 10 to over 30 per cent. In Yugoslavia and Romania, the share of agricultural manpower fell from 75–78 to between 57–60 per cent. In the middle tier of the area, the share of industry rose from 20–23 per cent in 1950 to 28–36 per cent in the early 1960's, while agriculture fell from 55–57 to 35–48 per cent. In the upper tier, the share of industrial employment rose only in Czechoslovakia; by the early 1960's, this share was of the order of 46–47 per cent of total employment; conversely, agriculture absorbed only from 16–23 per cent of available manpower.

While not all of the figures concerning employment are absolutely comparable, we can estimate that total industrial manpower rose by almost 70 per cent from 1950 to 1964, namely from some 8.2 million gainfully employed to over 13.8 million. Characteristically, a strong demand for new labor inputs and abundant manpower supplies led to rates of growth in employment higher than the average for the area in the less-developed countries, while, conversely, a more moderate demand for fresh labor inputs coupled with increasing labor shortages made the most developed countries register rates lower than the average.

Appreciable changes took place in the growth of various industries and in the structure of industrial manpower. Employment grew in absolute terms, but some leading industries increased their share in total industrial employment while other industries lost ground. Mining decreased in relative terms, compared to total manufacturing. Within manufacturing, the most spectacular growth occurred in the engineering industries; conversely, employment in textile and foodstuffs contracted, with one minor exception. Employment in engineering industries rose from 1.8 million in 1950 to over 3.8 million in 1964, or from 21.8 per cent of industrial employment to 27.8 per cent. Characteristically, in this leading branch as in industry as a whole, the highest rates of growth were registered in the lower and middle tiers, particularly in Poland. In 1950, the ratio of manpower in engineering to total industrial manpower fluctuated between 10–21 per cent in the less developed countries; 17–29 per cent in the middle tier; and 25–29 per cent in the upper tier. In 1964, these ratios had shifted to 18–25 per cent in the lower tier; 28–31 in the middle tier; and about 34 per cent in the upper tier.

INCREASING TECHNICAL MANPOWER

The expansion of employment in industry was accompanied by a systematic effort to increase the supply of high level manpower. In the early postwar years, the dearth of managers, engineers, and production leaders forced the new regimes to use available material. Party and trade union leaders were promoted and often placed in posts of leadership beyond their qualifications. By the end of the 1940's, it was clear that the manager had to be given more power in order to obtain increases in output and that a new and more competent strata of engineering-technical cadres or production leaders had to be developed quickly. In the perspective of the long-term plans, managerial responsibility and leadership were strengthened, and the role of the party cadres in the plans was curtailed. In addition, trade union leadership in the factory was turned away from management and production control, and instructed to transform itself into an "agitation instrument" for the fulfillment and overfulfillment of plan targets.

The problem of quickly creating a group of technical specialists became more pressing as plans for industrialization and development got underway. Former "bourgeois" specialists were often restored to positions of leadership. The formation of a technically trained elite was speeded by training workers on the job and by developing many types of technical schools. At the same time, a massive effort was undertaken for reducing illiteracy, increasing vocational and secondary-school training, developing accelerated evening programs, and expanding and diversifying graduate teaching, with emphasis on modern polytechnical schooling. Illiteracy fell significantly where it was most prevalent, and the supply of technically trained rose sharply. Technical talent was systematically developed in one-, two- or three-year vocational schools (based on eight-year elementary schools) and in four- or five-year secondary technical schools. The output of high level manpower to supply the needs of industry, transportation, education, and health increased substantially in each country. In short, the adaptation of education to "the needs of an increasingly industrialized and urbanized society" took in Eastern Europe forms "not unlike those necessitated by industrialization elsewhere in the world."

In the 1945-55 decade, the technical engineering cadres absorbed three groups: former technical specialists, technicians rising directly from the ranks of the Party, the trade unions, or the working class, and technicians newly trained in the secondary or higher level polytechnical schools. Since the late 1950's, the latter group has insistently backed its own candidates for positions of leadership. The London *Economist* of September 3, 1966 noted the increasing displacement "from the Baltic to the Black Sea" of former party executives "put out to grass" and their replacement by young engineers and business executives. The journal observed that the casualty rate in the managers' ranks would probably have been even "higher if there had been sufficient talent to fill the posts. . . . There may be sufficient qualified technicians, engineers and scientists. But efficient executives who can command with authority, read balance sheets and deal with labour problems are in desperate short supply."

Changing Inter-industry Relations

The multiple impacts of industrialization on inter-industry relations can best be followed through input-output tabulations registering the flows of sales and purchases of goods and services from industry to industry, from producers to distributors, then on to the final purchaser, the investor or the consumer. Crucial changes have taken place in the area in the relationship between the industrial and the agricultural sectors.

In order drastically to transform the previous demand-and-supply relationships between industry and agriculture and between the town and the countryside, the Communists carried out a swift and brutal reorganization of the peasantry throughout the 1950's. The processes of collectivization, which faltered only in Yugoslavia and Poland, involved a total of over 25 million gainfully employed in agriculture, along with their dependents. By the end of the 1950's, the "socialist" sector, the sector of state and collective farms, encompassed from 85–95 per cent of the total agricultural land of the area, except in Poland (13 per cent) and in Yugoslavia (somewhat less).

IMPACT OF COLLECTIVIZATION

Collectivization changed drastically the patterns of employment in the countryside, the share of marketed grain and animal produce (the bulk of which had to be delivered to the state under compulsory arrangements), and the input and output mixes in agriculture. Through formation of large land compounds, collectivization facilitated mechanization, particularly in the less developed countries. Between 1950 and 1964, the number of tractors in use rose sharply throughout the area. Mechanization accentuated, however, "disguised" unemployment in the countryside, and reduced appreciably the number of working hours needed in the collective per person per year. Since industry was unable to absorb the increasing surplus population on the farm, the peasant could find a partial outlet for his energies only in the more intense cultivation of the small plot of land, roughly one acre, alloted to him for his personal use. This displacement of the peasant by the machine and his increasing separation from the bulk of the collectivized agricultural land precipitated marked changes in the industrial inputs in agriculture and in the agricultural inputs in industry. As mechanization and chemical fertilization of the state and collectivized farms increased, the demand for machinery, spare parts, oil, and chemicals increased; on the other hand, as industry progressed and diversified its outputs, notably of artificial fibers, plastics, and related materials, its demand for flax, wool, cotton, skin and hides decreased relatively.

CHANGES WITHIN AGRICULTURE

Typically, the shares of agricultural deliveries to other industries and to final demand both increase when the level of development increases, though the relative importance of agricultural inputs in total industrial inputs decreases. The available data for Eastern Europe show that the shares of total agricultural output delivered at the end of the 1950's for further processing by industry were as follows: Yugoslavia, 17.6 per cent; Bulgaria, 24.4 per cent; Hungary, 27.6 per cent; Poland, 33.4 per cent; U.S.S.R., 39.7 per cent; and East Germany, 45.7 per cent. Normally, as technology reduces the farmers' demand for agricultural inputs, more is available for further processing and final demand. The share of final demand amounted to 25.8 per cent in Poland; 37.2 per cent in the U.S.S.R.; 37.4 per cent in Hungary; and 43.3 per cent in East Germany. This share was higher in Bulgaria and Yugoslavia, 51.9 and 53.8 per cent, respectively, but deliveries for processing to industry were lowest in these countries.

Mechanization may seem absurd in the presence of large surpluses of peasant manpower, and increased mechanization in the absence of sufficient employment opportunities can mean only further increases in manpower surplus. No intermediate way has been found in the less developed countries which allows achievement of both increases in output per acre and, at the same time, increases in output per head, and hence achievement of a decent standard of living in the villages.

Technology has made significant progress throughout the area, although all these countries remain far below Western standards. Even in East Germany, 45 hectares of agricultural land per tractor were in use in the mid-1960's, as against 8 hectares in West Germany, and 168 kg. of fertilizer were used per hectare, as against 186 kg. per hectare. In the rest of the area, mechanization and fertilizer use per hectare was considerably less in the middle and the lower tiers. Yields were correspondingly lower. All official Eastern European sources stress that a modern agriculture capable of meeting the needs of an expanding population and a growing industry is inconceivable without a high degree of mechanization, intensive use of chemicals, and expanded storage and transportation facilities. Investment in agricultural mechanization and chemical fertilizers has been relatively small because of the emphasis on heavy industry. All the Communist regimes remain committed in the long run to sustained efforts to increase output per acre via capital intensive methods, even at the risk of further deterioration in productivity per capita.

Growth in total agricultural output has remained low, as we noted. Poor planning, misallocation of resources, and inappropriate incentives have afflicted this sector. The new plans put more emphasis on the profitability of both state and collective farms, redress slightly the terms of trade between agriculture and industry in favor of the former, and aim to place the farms in a position where they can finance their own capital formation and expansion.

Foreign Trade

In order to stress properly the impact on foreign trade of the changes in inter-industry relations and output, one must note first that political elements of varying strength have affected both trade policies and practices since World War II. During the period from 1949–53, world trade was dominated by powerful tendencies toward trade compartmentalization into Eastern and Western blocs. During a second transitional period, from 1954–63, the Sino-Soviet bloc started to break up in various ways and, on the other hand, East-West interchanges began to multiply. Finally, a third period opened in the mid-1960's, which pointed toward increasing heterogeneity in planning and management under socialism and toward increasing opportunities for diversified East-West relations.

During the first period, a well-coordinated Western embargo on strategic goods interacted with strong centripetal tendencies in the foreign trade of the area. Each East European country was then tied to the U.S.S.R. by innumerable threads, and the Soviet Union easily dominated the intra-bloc market. In these circumstances, the East European countries lost their relative importance in world trade. As the second period got under way, the embargo decreased in both range and effectiveness, and the Soviet Union lost its previously unchallenged position in the bloc. Trade opportunities started to develop in the West for some East European countries, and the share of intra-bloc trade began to contract, hitting its lowest level in 1956. Soviet efforts to coordinate and integrate foreign trade and output plans in the area remained largely ineffective. After 1956, intra-bloc trade did expand again, but this time expansion was due to an increasingly sharp contraction in trade with China.

Since the mid-1960's, strong centrifugal tendencies have been developing in the foreign trade of these countries. East Germany and Czechoslovakia have been attempting to increase significantly their trade with the West. The middle tier countries have also tried to turn to the West, but their efforts have been far less successful and their dependence on the U.S.S.R. has become more pronounced. Finally, the less developed countries, excluding Yugoslavia and isolated Albania, are also trying to expand trade with the West (notably Germany and France), to diversify their ties with other less developed countries and to lessen their dependence on the U.S.S.R.

The structure and direction of foreign trade have been profoundly affected by the efforts of the developed countries of Eastern Europe to restructure industry in order to shift emphasis from consumer to capital goods, and of the less developed countries to industrialize on a large scale by emphasizing production of the intermediate products and capital goods needed to begin the transformation of the key branches of domestic industry. Structurally, trade with the West has not changed profoundly. Shifts occurring on the side of exports, from cereals and coal to oil, pig iron, and primarily timber, have affected in various degrees the earning capacity of the countries of the area, but the broad commodity structure has not been affected. As before the war, Eastern Europe, including the U.S.S.R., exports food, fuels and crude materials to the West, and imports steel, machinery and industrial equipment.

The impact of industrialization has made itself deeply felt, however, on the structure of the intra-East European, East European-Soviet, and East European-underdeveloped countries trade flows. Intra-East European trade and East European-Soviet trade in heavy equipment and machinery of all types, insignificant before the war, have appreciably grown and diversified. Trade among the members of the Council of Economic Mutual Assistance (COMECON or CEMA, comprised of the U.S.S.R., Mongolia, and all the East European countries except Albania and Yugoslavia) absorbed from 60–80 per cent of each other's machinery exports in the early 1960's. Machinery and equipment exports represent 45–48 per cent of the total exports of East Germany and Czechoslovakia; 28–38 per cent of the exports of Poland and Hungary; and 15–20 per cent of the exports of Bulgaria, Romania, and the U.S.S.R. In turn, machinery and equipment account for 12–21 per cent of the imports of East Germany and Czechoslovakia; about 27 per cent of Poland and Hungary; and 30–43 per cent of Bulgaria, Romania, and the Soviet Union. The U.S.S.R. remains the largest importer of machinery in the area and the biggest exporter of raw materials, particularly of iron ore, steel and oil. CEMA's exports toward the underdeveloped countries of the Middle East and other parts of the world have substantially grown and contain a significant amount of machinery and equipment.

From 1953 to the mid-1960's, over-all trade grew at the average rate of over 19 per cent per year; in Hungary and Bulgaria, the rate of growth has been even higher. While trade per capita remains low, the potential for further growth is certain. Per capita foreign trade ranged in the 1960's from a high of $365 for Czechoslovakia and $320 for East Germany to a low of $65 for the Soviet Union. Taking the average per capita trade for Eastern Europe and the U.S.S.R. as 100 for the early 1960's, the per capita average for the European Common Market is about 400 and that of the European Outer Seven (EFTA) about 485. Hence, the ratios of foreign trade to national income remain low in the area. In 1964, they were probably 8–9 per cent for the U.S.S.R.; 16–18 per cent for Romania and Poland; and from 22–30 per cent for the other countries.

Economic Fluctuations and System Redesigning

THE SOVIET MODEL AND ITS CONSEQUENCES

By imitating Soviet centralized planning and management and by applying Soviet strategy and its emphases, the Communist regimes sought to achieve both rapid growth in certain leading sectors and rapid and sustained growth in total and per capita product. The Soviet system of centralized management and of directive or "command" planning (setting specific physical targets for each sector, branch, and plant; earmarking at the source the physical output shares to be invested and consumed; and determining rigorously the the pattern of allocation of the goods produced) was supposed to prevent cyclical fluctuations, avoid unemployment and other wastage of resources, and achieve consistently high over-all rates of growth.

These regimes earmarked high shares of investment, generously allocated resources to preferential sectors and branches, introduced the most up-to-date technology in the privileged military and industrial establishments, and achieved remarkable results in these leading sectors. But centralized management and command planning could not prevent economic fluctuations, wastage of resources in innumerable forms, and falling rates of growth in total product. Even the official data, no matter how deficient they are, clearly show these facts. Thus, the data available on investment, industrial output, and net material product point clearly toward two types of variations in the economic activity of all the countries of the area, particularly of the more developed ones: (a) cyclical variations, with peaks in 1950–52 and 1958–60, and troughs in the early 1950's and 1960's; and (b) long-term declines in the rate of growth, readily apparent when contrasting average annual growth rates during, say, 1950–60 and 1961–65.

Table 3: Annual Growth Rates of Net Material National Product, 1950-1960, 1961-1965, and Percentage Changes from Preceding Year, 1961-1965 (Official Data).

	Annual Averages		Percentage changes from preceding year.				
	1950-60*	1961-65**	1961	1962	1963	1964	1965
East Germany	8.0	2.8	3.5	2.2	2.9	4.5	4.7
Czechoslovakia	7.7	1.9	6.8	1.4	−2.2	0.9	2.5
Hungary	6.5	4.6	6.1	4.7	5.7	4.7	2
Poland	7.8	6.9	8.2	2.1	6.9	6.6	6
Bulgaria	9.2	6.5	2.8	6.2	7.5	9.9	6
Romania	10.5	9.0	10.0	4.0	10.0	11.0	8
Yugoslavia	10.0	—	—	—	—	—	—
Albania	9.1	7.3	5.8	8.0	8.0	4	3

* 1955-60 for East Germany; 1952-1960 for Bulgaria and Yugoslavia.
** 1959-65 for East Germany; 1960-65 for Romania, 1960-64 for Albania.

SOURCES: United Nations, *The Growth of World Industry, 1938-1961* (New York, 1963), *passim;* United Nations, *Economic Survey of Europe in 1965* (New York, 1966), 3; United Nations, *Yearbook of National Accounts Statistics,* 1965 (New York, 1966), 474-475.

The fluctuations in the annual growth rates of investment are traceable to a number of factors, particularly to differences in output patterns and growth rates within the privileged sectors, as between manufacturing as a whole on the one hand and mining on the other; differences in demand for capital equipment and labor, as between the various privileged industries and the non-privileged ones; and distortions in allocations due to over-emphasis on investment in industries requiring long periods of maturation. Other important factors include unpredictable distortions in allocation and use of investible resources due to an administratively manipulated price structure; unforeseen fluctuations due to technical and organizational shortcomings, leading to discrepancies in supply and demand and in project completion; changing armament and defense requirements; and strong impacts of foreign trade fluctuations, particularly in the more developed countries.

The fluctuations in investment affected, in turn, the rates of growth in total product and its main component, the industrial output. The trends in the annual growth rates of both net material product and gross industrial output show a characteristically cyclical pattern, along with a declining overall trend. The official data on annual growth rates of the net material product show negative growth rates in 1954 and 1956 for a number of these countries and unusually low rates of growth for the others. A similar Soviet decline in the early 1960's was finally noticed in the West as an extraordinary phenomenon, although in fact it was simply a recurring dip affecting both Soviet and East European growth.

In contrast to these sharp cyclical fluctuations, the cyclical variations were much less violent in the West. Western stability was due largely to far more sophistication in anticyclical policy and to improved utilization of fiscal and monetary instruments. Perceiving only dimly the causes of the gyrations of their economies and lacking adequate monetary and fiscal policies and instruments necessary for advanced industrial economies, the managers of the centralized planned economies of Eastern Europe were incapable of counteracting effectively the cyclical pushes. The crises of the early 1960's made these facts more apparent than ever before. Under these conditions, the question of system redesigning (searching for new patterns of planning and management) gained momentum throughout Eastern Europe.

New Systems of Management and Planning

The patent inefficiency of a highly centralized planning and management system has been illustrated by declining growth rates, the development of cumbersome and inflexible planning machinery, the disintegration of the system of incentives, and deterioration in the levels of living. These manifestations have accented the need for a change from detailed central commands to decentralized structures. As the search began for new patterns of management and planning, new consideration was given to the use of monetary instruments in a centrally guided economy. Everything related to fiscal and monetary policies and instruments, prices, business accounting, banking and credit, and taxation, suddenly acquired an importance previously unknown in Soviet and East European economic thinking. The crux of the matter is the question of prices, of course. How should the distorted price structure be straightened out so as to reflect scarcities, without impinging upon key central decisions? What criteria should be used in coping with the broader issues of efficiency in the allocation of investment, its sectoral distribution, and the length of its recoupment periods? How should the banking system and credit be used to increase investment responsibility at the operational levels and avoid dispersal and wastage of investable resources? How can consumers' preferences influence production without impinging upon the main directions set for the economy in the long run?

These are some of the problems which now confront the East European policy makers, managers, and planners. The beginnings of what might be called the era of New Economic Management point toward increasing pragmatism in the solutions to be adopted. Undoubtedly, the pioneering efforts of Yugoslavia after its expulsion from the Soviet bloc have exercised a deep impact on the other countries of the area. However, it is not the so-called market socialism model of Yugoslavia or the highly decentralized Yugoslav system based on the self-management of all enterprises which serves as model, but rather the Western type of corporate society, with highly concentrated large-scale enterprises under the guidance of a powerful board of directors. The Western model, which was first adopted in the early 1960's by the East Germans, is now being emulated and adapted throughout Eastern Europe.

The cornerstone of the new system of management is the national enterprise, trust, or concern; it is not the center which will henceforth command the output patterns, the input norms and, eventually, the prices of the goods produced by big national enterprises. As in the French system, planning will become a "game" in which a number of agents of national stature, besides the Central Planning Board, will be the "players." Their interaction will establish a pliable, adjustable, long-term planning framework to be revised each year. Thus it is not Yugoslav practice and economic thought which are influencing changes in the East; it is Western theory, methods, and techniques in both economics and in management.

The reduction of the Party's role in production, the changing scope of planning, and the strengthened voice of the consumer will eventually have to be combined with the sharp curtailment of the system of physical allocation of raw materials, with price liberalizations, and ultimately, with the expansion of the authority of management to include the right of dealing with the bulk of investments without serious interference from the center. It is, however, as yet not entirely foreseeable to what extent and in which specific forms each East European country will move in this direction.

Conclusions

Communist Eastern Europe is the world's fourth industrial complex, following the United States, the U.S.S.R., and Western Europe, and preceding Japan. This achievement reflects the inclusion of East Germany in the Communist-ruled economies of East Europe, the restructuring of the East German and the Czechoslovakian economies, and the significant advances in industrialization made by the other countries of the area. With a total population of over 120 million in the mid-1960's, an industrial labor force of over 14 million, a total crude steel output of over 30 million tons, an electric power output of over 170 billion kwh, a variety of modern machinery and armament outputs, and a foreign trade total of close to $25 billion per year, Eastern Europe (including Yugoslavia) has become an important producer of and market for both industrial and agricultural products.

However, wide differences in levels of development still exist between the older industrialized countries, such as East Germany and Czechoslovakia, and the other countries. These differences are difficult, if not impossible, to bridge. Comparison of average income levels for the area with Western averages is misleading. The industrialized countries of the area's upper tier are close to Western Europe's levels, but the less developed countries are still far behind. The backwardness of the Polish, Romanian and Yugoslav villages still represents an enormous dead weight left by the past on the shoulders of the present and the future.

The pace of growth in gross national product was particularly rapid in the years 1950-52 and 1958-60, and more rapid than in the West over the decade of the 1950's as a whole. On the other hand, growth has been erratic from year to year, and the inefficiencies of the centralized planning system copied from the U.S.S.R. have been costly. The pace of growth in industrial output has been more rapid in Eastern than in Western Europe in the 1950's and about of the same order of magnitude in the early 1960's. These increases have been due both to capital deepening and to massive absorption of labor, particularly in the less developed countries. The productivity gains, on the other hand, have been erratic and far slower in these countries than in the advanced countries. The increases in the engineering industries have been spectacular, though duplication is widespread and the output scale, limited by domestic requirements, is inefficient.

The pace of growth in agriculture has been much slower than in the West. Wide and brutal social and institutional rearrangements, precipitated by political expediency rather than by calculated economic objectives, have alienated the peasantry. The land reforms of the late 1940's, which gave small plots of land to the peasant, and the collectivization of the late 1950's, which took these plots away in order to create the large land compounds needed for mechanization, have hardly won the enthusiasm of the villages. Poland, which needed the support of the peasants for colonizing the western territories taken from the Germans, and Yugoslavia have not collectivized the countryside. However, barring unforeseeable changes in the regime's philosophy, Poland will probably try to renew its collectivization drive in the 1970's. Massive mechanization cannot rest on the shoulders of individual farmers when these farmers cannot accumulate large reserves of capital. Modern agriculture is big business, and investments of tens of thousands of dollars are required even for a farm of 300 acres.

The pace of growth in services, except those directly connected to production (transportation of freight, communications, wholesale distributing and storing facilities), has been extremely slow. Everything connected with the consumer, production of consumers' goods, assortment, quality, distribution, housing, commercial and personal services, has been neglected in order to further capital goods output. Investment in human beings has been reduced primarily to investment in education, and the amenities associated with modern living have been neglected. The progress of a sharply restructured educational system, perhaps much too much inclined toward polytechnical training, has, however, been significant and has laid a sound basis for future growth.

The spread of modern technology throughout the economy has been severely limited by rigid emphasis on the privileged industrial branches. Obsolescence and inefficiency in the nonprivileged branches have increased as industrialization on the Soviet model has proceeded. Resistances to change-overs in production from old to new methods has hampered, on the other hand, even the rapid spread of up-to-date technology in the privileged branches. Technical cooperation, which has developed among the countries of the CEMA group, has facilitated access to advanced production techniques for the less developed countries and has benefited even the advanced countries themselves. But this practice is coming to a close as a variety of centrifugal tendencies break up the formerly cohesive Soviet bloc.

The advances made in technology have not been on a par with those which have taken place in the West. Because of a strategic embargo banning the export of certain Western goods, the East German and the Czechoslovakian industries enjoyed for a while a sheltered, monopolistic position on the East European markets for machinery and equipment of all types. As the embargo has been drawing to a close and as East Germany and Czechoslovakia have been forced to compete more aggressively on the East European markets with Western products, the inferiority in technology and quality of their products has become increasingly apparent. Thus, even the most advanced countries of the area risk falling behind the fast-moving technological progress which is taking place in the West, unless they break out of their isolation, expand their contacts with the advanced Western markets, and remove the barriers to the spread of modern technology within their own economies.

East European agricultural technology is, of course, lagging even more than industry behind the revolutions achieved in the West. The transformation of agriculture into the Communist ideal of "factories in the fields" is a long process and very costly. There is a long way from mechanizing plowing, seeding, and harvesting to mechanizing animal output and developing modern methods for feeding, milking, refrigerating, and storing. The way is even longer to the massive use of chemicals in agriculture and to the achievement of genetic revolutions in plant and livestock rearing.

An American agricultural expert, Ronald L. Mighell, noted in a book published in the 1950's that four periods are distinguishable in the recent development of agricultural technology. The first, covering the first half of the nineteenth century, was the period of the axe and hoe. The second, covering the latter half of the nineteenth century, was the period of horsedrawn machinery. The third, covering the first half of the twentieth century, was the period of mechanical power. The fourth, beginning in the second half of the twentieth century, is the period of the chemical and genetic revolutions. In the Communist world, China is still largely in the first and, at best, in the second of these periods; the less developed countries of Eastern Europe are only engaging in the third phase and barely approaching, in a very limited way, the fourth period. Their model, the U.S.S.R., is still far from having achieved massive mechanization of agriculture; Eastern Europe's less developed countries are even further back.

The introduction of modern technology in services has been extremely slow. Both modernization of distribution and increased access of the consumer to modern appliances, radios, television, and cars are still to come. According to various estimates, if per capita personal consumption in Western Germany is taken as equal to 100, the consumption per capita in the upper East European tier could be equated to 60 per cent; in the middle tier to 50 per cent; and in the lower tier to 40 per cent and less. While progress in the West accelerates in this respect, Eastern Europe is following far behind.

Efforts to achieve better allocation of investable resources are hampered by difficulties in management and planning concepts and methods and by traditional historical distrusts and conflicting interests. The duplication and misallocation of resources have not been avoided, notwithstanding the efforts made by the U.S.S.R. and the CEMA countries for integrating their foreign trade and some of their output plans. The harsh and short-sighted way in which the Russians treated Eastern Europe in the Stalinist era has not prepared the U.S.S.R. for the role of disinterested arbiter of a united "socialist common market." Centrifugal tendencies are strong in the area as a whole, the U.S.S.R. still dominates the area economically, and East Germany, Czechoslovakia, Hungary and Poland in particular remain dependent on Soviet supplies of raw materials and markets for industrial goods. Distrust exists, not only between Eastern Europe as a whole and the U.S.S.R., but also among the East European countries themselves. Old conflicts are grafted on new divergent interests, like the traditional Hungarian-Romanian conflict over Transylvania, now embittered by the fact that Romania opposes Hungarian sharing in the exploitation of the rich raw material resources of the province, particularly natural gas. While Hungary is starved of raw materials, the Romanians "sit" on the Transylvanian resources, waiting for the time when they alone will be able to put them to full use.

* * *

It is too early to draw the balance sheet of the results achieved in furthering modern economic growth under Communist rule. It is, however, clear that the Communists have rooted out certain old barriers to economic growth, changed values and outlook, and succeeded in institutionalizing a high rate of investment, an indispensable ingredient for growth. On the other hand, the Communists have erected new and formidable barriers to development, thanks to their rigid, wasteful and often patently incompetent leadership; their questionable set of investment priorities, targets and commitments; their distorted incentives; and their dogmatic approaches to the crucial problem of development, namely, the relationship between industry and agriculture. Changes are now in process in planning, management and incentives; but no one can venture to tell how long it will take the Communists to destroy the barriers they themselves have created.

R. V. Burks

4

Social Forces and Cultural Change

Eastern Europe has throughout history been unusually subject to cultural influences coming from the outside. Various sections
of the region, for example, have been ruled for many centuries by
outsiders; by Greeks, by Turks, by Italians, by Austrians, by Russians. These external rulers have not only exerted their own cultural
influence, but frequently they and their cultures have also contended
with each other for domination of the area.

This contention is most fruitfully exemplified for the purposes of
the present chapter by the conversion of Eastern Europe to Christianity in the ninth and tenth centuries. Catholic Christianity was
introduced from the north and west by German monks, backed by
German knights. Orthodox Christianity was brought in from the
south and east by Greek monks, who had the support of Byzantine
soldiers. The two sponsoring powers, the Germanic empire in Western Europe and the Byzantine empire in the Near East, saw in the
conversion of the East European peoples to their particular brand
of Christianity the creation of allied or satellite peoples.

The boundary between Orthodoxy and Catholicism continues to
divide the populations of Eastern Europe. The consequences of that
division are strikingly illustrated by the long-standing quarrel be-

R. V. Burks *is professor of history at Wayne State University and former
policy director of Radio Free Europe in Munich. He is the author of,
among other books,* Dynamics of Communism in Eastern Europe.

tween the Serbs and the Croats, who speak an identical language
and have been neighbors from time immemorial. But the Serbs are
Orthodox and look to the East for help and inspiration, whereas the
Croats are Catholic and look to the West. Peace between these two
peoples is very difficult to keep, as even the Communist rulers of
contemporary Yugoslavia can testify.

Despite the continuing influx of competing foreign cultural influences, or perhaps because of it, the peoples of Eastern Europe have
developed distinct national personalities and highly articulated national cultures. The Slovenes of Yugoslavia may serve as an example.
This Slavic population was conquered by the Germans in the ninth
century, their landed aristocracy being destroyed in the process, and
for centuries Slovene literature existed as an oral tradition only.
However, in the nineteenth century, after a thousand years of German rule, the Slovenes developed an intelligentsia of their own,
together with grammars, dictionaries, and a written literature. The
Slovenes today form one of the six republics of Yugoslavia, but their
devotion to their language, their literature, their Catholic Church,
and their national traditions is stronger than in the past. What is
true of the Slovenes is true, *mutatis mutandis,* of the other ten peoples of Eastern Europe, from the Poles, with a present population
of more than thirty-one million to the Montenegrins, of whom there
are only a few hundred thousand.

It should be clear, then, that the attempt of the German Nazis in
the course of World War II to impose their brand of culture on the
peoples of Eastern Europe and the subsequent domination of these
peoples by the Soviet Russians were not new experiences for the
subject populations. Moreover, the demonstrated ability of these
populations to cling to their own cultures in the face of massive
oppression should have produced confidence in their ultimate resurgence under Communism. These cultures in revival will naturally
have been affected by both the Nazis and the Soviets; each of the
conquerors will have left a cultural deposit, as did the Ottoman
Turks, the Byzantine Greeks, and the Catholic Germans. But these
Nazi and Soviet deposits in the long run will be only elements in a
larger whole. In the following pages, we will discuss successively the
efforts of the Russians to transform the national cultures of Eastern
Europe, the counter forces both indigenous and exogenous which
developed in the course of this effort, and finally the resurgence of
the national cultures.

The Effort at Sovietization: 1944-1956

The cultural policy which the Russians sought to impose on Eastern Europe was both a reflection and a counterpart of the cultural policy pursued in the Soviet Union itself by the Bolshevik party under Stalin. In its bare essentials, Stalin's over-all policy after World War II sought simultaneously the rapid reconstruction of the U.S.S.R., which had been devastated by the German invasion, and a great new revolutionary advance, the first step of which was occupation and transformation of part of Germany and most of Eastern Europe. Implementation of this over-all policy involved imposing further heavy sacrifices on a Soviet population which had gone through the forced industrialization of 1928-1941 and the Nazi invasion.

During the first years of Soviet domination, 1944-1956, the states of Eastern Europe were treated as if they were members of the Union of Socialist Soviet Republics. The peculiar form of government set up by the Communists in Eastern Europe, the so-called people's democracy, was defined as a dictatorship of the proletariat in content but not in form. The East European Communist parties accepted their policies from Moscow. The substance of their task was the reconstruction and rapid industrialization of Eastern Europe so that the area might process Soviet raw materials and add to Soviet military potential. To make sure that Soviet policies were implemented, satellite security police, armies, and planning agencies were supplied with Soviet advisors. Those assigned to the police were undoubtedly the most important, since the policies imposed by Stalin required so much popular sacrifice that only systematic use of police terror and forced labor camps ensured that they be carried out.

The cultural aspects of Soviet policy were particularly the work of Andrei A. Zhdanov, and are usually referred to as the Zhdanov line or Zhdanovism. Cultural Zhdanovism involved three fundamentals. First, all writers and artists throughout the Soviet empire, including Eastern Europe, were to employ their talents exclusively in the service of rapid industrialization and new revolutionary advance. Second, Western living standards were to be minimized and Western culture denigrated. This involved reducing contact with the West to the vanishing point, by erection of an iron curtain and persecution of both Catholics and Jews. Third, and this phase of the Zhdanov line applied with special force in Eastern Europe, Russian culture was to serve as the model and the Russian language was to become the *lingua franca* of the whole area. The achievement of this aim necessitated a major shift in the organization and curricula of the Eastern educational systems.

SOCIALIST REALISM

The central theme of Socialist Realism, in Russia as well as Eastern Europe, was the creation of the new Socialist man, a being who would shed the selfishness of bourgeois society and be motivated solely by the common good. Socialist man was bound to emerge as society approached a classless state. Writers and artists were to hasten the day by communicating to the public a sense of optimism in the face of grave difficulties and by presenting a series of positive heroes to serve as models. Novels were written, for example, dealing with the local party bureaucrat who persuaded his factory hands to over-fulfill their production quota in the face of incredible obstacles. Paintings revealed the Great Stalin in white party uniform, surrounded by admiring legislators and beaming benignly on all. Music was produced and performed only if it were easily understood by the masses and inculcated a spirit of optimism and triumph.

Socialist Realism was also a device for controlling the creative activity of the East European intelligentsia. The party ideologues established the line in literature and the arts, and the writers, painters, and composers were then ordered to fulfill their particular assignments. This kind of "guidance" in literature and the arts also functioned as a kind of pre-censorship; this was more effective as a means of control than the traditional censorship of the completed work, although that kind of censorship continued to exist also.

Nonetheless, the writers and artists experienced great difficulty in implementing the line to the satisfaction of the political authorities. This was partly because the line often changed by the time a novel was completed, but it was mainly because the party sought the impossible: creativity which was both uncritical and ran counter to the cultural tradition. What the writers published was anodyne in character, dull and uninteresting hack work. In Eastern Europe, Socialist Realism, as in the Soviet Union, inspired hardly a single novel, play, painting, or musical composition worth remembering.

Many writers and artists in fact led a double life. In addition to their regular work which was their means of earning a living, they also wrote "for the drawer." Many novels, short stories, and poems circulated only in manuscript form. Painters who were forbidden to use such styles as cubism or surrealism would paint for their own satisfaction and store the paintings. When the Stalinist system started to disintegrate, after the death of the dictator in 1953, it did so first in the field of Socialist Realism. Writers and artists began to disregard the canons of that doctrine in their public creations. "The thaw" took place in the Soviet Union also, but it went faster and further in two of the satellite countries, Poland and Hungary. The Hungarian uprising of October 1956, and the peaceful Polish upheaval of the same month cannot be understood except as products of this ferment and criticism among the intellectuals.

THE IRON CURTAIN

Zhdanovism involved the lowering of an iron curtain. Actually, there were two iron curtains. The physical iron curtain, composed of watch towers, barbed wire, mine fields, and trigger-happy sentinels stretched like a great evil snake from the Danish frontier in the north to the Greek frontier in the south. It was through this iron curtain that political fugitives sought to escape at the risk of their very lives.

A spiritual iron curtain, a veil of censorship, jamming, and supervised travel not only minimized cultural contact with the outside world but also isolated the East European peoples from each other. The rare visitor to Eastern Europe in these times noticed at once the absence of the Western press, except for occasional copies of Communist papers. The only news available was that in the local one-party press, which was hardly news at all. The press and the radio were full of long verbatim speeches of party leaders, pledges by this factory or that mine to fulfill and overfulfill its quota in honor of a party congress, and the inevitable editorial providing the party line. The fare was exceedingly dull.

Some fortunate East European citizens were able to listen to the news or to editorial comment from varying points of view on the Western radio. This was virtually impossible in the larger cities, because ground-wave jammers secretly stationed every few blocks simply blotted out the signal. Even in the countryside, however, less effective sky-wave jamming operated, mostly from transmitters located in the U.S.S.R. itself. In no country was it against the law to listen to the Western radio, but all had laws forbidding the spreading of false rumors, i.e., information garnered from the Western radio.

The mass media were not the only intellectual fare denied the East Europeans. Except in such fields as physics and mathematics, the learned journals of the West were unavailable. Novels written outside the iron curtain were virtually unknown, with the exception of those highly critical of the West, which were, of course, translated and published in mass editions. Western films were few in number. The only Western plays produced were classics such as Shakespeare or Moliere. Foreigners were discouraged from going to Eastern Europe. The few tourists were usually accompanied by trusted guides. As a rule, an East European intellectual could go abroad only as a member of an official delegation. Writing for publication in the West was, of course, strictly forbidden.

The spiritual iron curtain was drawn not only between East and West and between the East European populations, but also between the present and the past. The cultural achievements of the national past were declared tainted with Fascism, chauvinism, capitalism, or Christianity. The national classics were printed only in small editions. New history books provided a Marxist-Leninist interpretation of the national past, and the works of inconvenient national heroes, such as Thomas G. Masaryk, founder of the Czechoslovak state, were declared alien. In non-Slavic nations, such as Romania and Hungary, the role of Slavic influence was exaggerated.

In short, the iron curtain was designed to interrupt cultural communication between the peoples of Eastern Europe, to keep these peoples and those of the West apart, and to separate the national past from the present. The Soviets hoped that the peoples of Eastern Europe could thus be brought to believe what they otherwise would not credit and to cherish what they might otherwise despise, i.e., to accept a way of life which was at the same time new, totalitarian, and alien.

PERSECUTION OF THE CHURCHES

In the period of sovietization, the churches of Eastern Europe were subjected to steady pressure from state authorities and to outright persecution. The Orthodox churches suffered least. They were nationally organized and had no formal connection either with each other or with the outside world. In addition, they had a long tradition of strict subordination to the secular authorities. Nonetheless, the Orthodox churches did suffer. Worship was not prevented, but the income from the state was reduced; monasteries were closed; it was difficult to get permission to repair churches, much less to build them; and the official view clearly emphasized that the church belonged to a by-gone era.

The situation of the Catholic church was more difficult, in part because of its international character, in part because some of the clergy had collaborated with extremist elements of the right. Thus, the Fascist regime of Ante Pavelic in Croatia, 1940-1944, had drawn major support from the Catholic clergy. In countries with large Catholic populations, the heads of the church and many of their bishops were arrested and imprisoned. Episcopal sees were left vacant for many years because the regimes refused to agree to successors. Communication with Rome was prohibited or reduced to a bare minimum. Competitive organizations of renegade priests, usually referred to officially as patriotic priests, were set up under regime sponsorship. Ecclesiastical charity was severely circumscribed, and catechetical instruction on church property was made difficult or prevented.

However, it was not the Christian but the Jew who suffered most. The loyalty of Jewish party members was put in question in the minds of Stalin and Zhdanov because of the foundation in 1948 of the state of Israel. However, the great bulk of the Jews who had survived the Nazi holocaust were non-Communist and many, if not most, of these preferred emigration to citizenship. This was embarrassing to the Communists, especially since the Jewish population contained a high proportion of the professionals whose services were badly needed for industrialization. Finally, East European politicians had traditionally turned the ire of the masses against the Jews, especially in times of great stress.

As a consequence, synagogues were closed, or fell into disrepair. Unleavened bread for passover and new prayer books could not be obtained, and books and newspapers in Yiddish or Hebrew were prohibited. Emigration was forbidden, though a few thousand Jews managed to escape. Jews in general were treated as hostile foreigners. In Hungary, Czechoslovakia, and Romania, Communist Jews were slaughtered by the hundred, sometimes after a sham public trial. The Sephardic Jews south of the Danube were in general not mistreated, and Communist Poland also proved an exception.

EDUCATIONAL CHANGE

A structural reform of the educational systems of Eastern Europe ran parallel to the policies of Socialist Realism, cultural isolationism, and religious persecution. The educational systems had been much like those in Western Europe. Broadly speaking, of course, educational opportunities were not so great in Eastern as in Western Europe, nor were academic levels so high. This was especially true in the south and east. In contrast to the American school system, the European schools were distinguished by the imposition of heavy scholarly burdens on school children, by a sharply marked double-track system for separating future professionals from skilled workers, by great emphasis upon the study of mathematics and foreign languages, and by less intensive training at the graduate level. The general effect of sovietization on education was to lower standards while increasing enrollments, to downgrade the humanities and the social sciences in favor of engineering and technical skills, to introduce a systematic Party view into all areas of instruction, and to subordinate all education to strict political control.

Industrialization of course requires a greatly expanded professional and technical class, so university enrollments inevitably increased greatly and an increased proportion of the students came from poorer homes. The Communists, however, made an ideological virtue of this change, giving preference in admission to applicants who came from worker or peasant families. When most applicants of lower class origin proved not to possess the required qualifications, standards were lowered. Academic standards also declined because the student body was so often required to assist in such undertakings as harvesting or building railway spurs.

Russian language was introduced into curricula as a virtually universal requirement, while Soviet literature, Soviet science, and Soviet achievements were in general given heavy emphasis. Economics, political theory, and philosophy were taught, but only from a Marxist-Leninist point of view. Courses in sociology, where they had existed, were dropped. The instruction and practice of psychiatry passed under a cloud, Pavlovian psychology being given the official imprimatur.

The Marxist-Leninist position in psychology is instructive. Pavlov was a major hero to the Communists, not only because he was one of the few Russians to have won a Nobel prize, but more especially because he appeared to have demonstrated, in a series of famous experiments with dogs, that all human behaviour was built up from the conditioning of simple reflex actions. This the Bolsheviks took as scientific confirmation of their materialist view that man is shaped entirely by his physical environment, and that in revolutionizing this environment the Bolsheviks would create a new type of human being, whom they called Socialist man. Freud, on the other hand, was anathema to the Marxist-Leninists because the psychology created by this Viennese physician depicted man as a highly subjective being driven by irrational forces; some suspected also that many Communists opposed psychiatry because they stood in personal fear of it.

In addition, the universities were shackled with a degree of political control new even in their experience. The faculties lost their voice in the selection of rectors and deans. Professors whose competence was without question but whose political views were suspect were provided assistants who belonged to the party and who reported to the police. Candidates for degrees usually faced two examinations, one in the substantive field, and the other in Marxism-Leninism. The university branch of the national organization of Communist youth played a major role in the life of each institution. It usually controlled the allocation of dormitory space, and it often had a voice in faculty appointments and the granting of degrees.

Counter-Forces and Counter-Trends: 1950-1967

The East Europeans naturally resisted sovietization of their national cultures. As long as Stalin lived and the Communists ruled by terror, the subject populations bent with the political wind, as centuries of experience had taught them to do. However, when Stalin died, and his successors attempted to rule by means of persuasion and material incentives, which Khrushchev called "goulash Communism," and to abandon police terror as a regular instrument of governance, the East European populations began to press for change. Meantime, it turned out that the Communists had inadvertently given hostages to their subjects. The policy of rapid industrialization had brought about social changes in Eastern Europe which themselves undermined the intended effects of sovietization.

Moreover, at the same time, the unity and discipline of the Communist Bloc began to break down. The emergence by 1961 of an open quarrel between the two major Communist powers, the Soviet Union and China, and the development of that quarrel into a

schism frayed the discipline of the international Communist movement and gave each regime increased opportunity. Thus, Albania,
fearing that she might be sacrificed to Yugoslavia as part of the
rapprochement between Belgrade and Moscow, switched orbits in
1961 and became a Chinese satellite. Romania, faced with Soviet
refusal to help or even to permit her industrialization, chose the
path of defiance and undertook to industrialize by importing machinery from the West. The disruption of Bloc unity created an
environment highly favorable to national differentiation along cultural lines.

THE NEW CLASS

The most important of the internal changes was the emergence of
what Milovan Djilas, the Yugoslav heretic, called the new class. This
was an inevitable by-product of industrialization, but it was also a
result of Communist totalitarianism, which subjected every aspect
of life to scrutiny and control and produced a phenomenal expansion of the bureaucracy.

In one sense, the new class was not new. Many of its component
elements had been part of the old ruling class: the intelligentsia, the
body of writers and artists whose influence in Eastern Europe has
traditionally been political; an elite of managers, engineers, and
accountants who had been immediately responsible for the operation
of industry; the professional bureaucracy; the army officers' corps;
and a greatly expanded security police. What was new about the
composition of the new class was that it also included the party
apparatus as its decision-making constituent, and that it excluded
such traditional elite groups as the landed aristocracy, the capitalists,
and the higher clergy.

The new class was not only more numerous than the former
ruling group, but it was also more heavily proletarian and peasant in
origin. It was less well educated and less well trained, partly as a
result of the lowering of university standards and the general poli-
ticization of the educational system, and partly because of a policy
which rated political loyalty above professional qualification. The
new class was also ethnically more homogeneous. There were, for
example, few ethnic Germans in high places in Hungary or Bohemia,
and a smaller number of Jewish professionals in Poland or Eastern
Germany.

Despite intensive indoctrination, the new class was only superficially Communist, in any sense of belief or ideology. Many of its

members, perhaps the majority, were opportunists, professionals who had joined the Communist Party to pursue their careers, or former Fascists looking for security. So many careerists joined that the Party had to organize special courses and even special schools to acquaint the new members with the elementary teachings of Marxism-Leninism. In short, the new class was very bourgeois in its outlook and motivation. It behaved very much as the *nouveau riche* in a capitalist country, crassly concerned with apartments, refrigerators, private automobiles, and dachas. Moreover, most members of the new class had an ingrained belief in the superiority of the capitalist West and in the "europeanness," if we may coin a term, of Eastern Europe. They were made uncomfortable by censorship and by the restrictions on foreign travel, and they abhorred the use of police terror as a method of government.

At the same time, the new class believed in the new system as a going concern, even if they did not believe in Communism. It took pride in what had been accomplished in industrialization, and it accepted state ownership of industry, extensive social security, and free university education. It felt that it had been rightfully given the country to manage, if not to govern. But it was also confident that it could direct more effectively if the Russians would not interfere. There was downright resentment of Soviet exploitation through reparations, joint companies, and differential prices. This resentment varied in intensity from country to country, but the new class in each country tended to be highly patriotic, if not chauvinistic, in its outlook.

THE YOUTH

The new middle class harbored grave doubts about many features of the Stalinist system; East European youth tended to reject it altogether. Despite heavy indoctrination, careful regimentation, and free university education, the Communists had failed to capture the oncoming generation. The young people, at least superficially, rejected both capitalism and Socialism. Youth was not trapped by the propaganda of the regime about Socialism, because the realities were before its very eyes. At the same time, youth was disinclined to believe that conditions under capitalism were significantly better. Their rejection of Socialism took two forms: extensive participation in hooligan activities, and open defiance of the regimes in the matter of tastes important to them. In particular, they were impressed by Western popular music, jazz above all.

The wide-spread character of hooliganism had a social explanation. Large-scale employment of women in an effort to maximize
industrial growth rates left children without proper supervision or
care after school. The acute shortage of urban housing, the result of
war-time destruction, of a vast influx of peasants into urban centers,
and of the regimes' concentration on the growth of heavy industry,
created a situation in which there was approximately one room per
family, and the count included bedrooms, living rooms, and kitchens.
Although the situation has improved somewhat, the shortage of
housing continues to make family life difficult and to propel youngsters onto the street. However, hooliganism in the streets is also a
political phenomenon, a protest against the conditions which produced it and against excessive regimentation, lying propaganda, and
the drabness of everyday life.

Jazz music offers a relief from the boredom and fatigue of Socialism and a means of defying the regime. Zhdanov had forbidden jazz
as a corrupt and decadent by-product of capitalism. Regime radios
and night clubs were forbidden to play jazz; broadcasts of jazz music
from the West were jammed; jazz records were prohibited. Eastern
European youth and Western broadcasters therefore concluded an
alliance. Youth obtained tape recorders and organized amateur
jazz combos. The broadcasters provided the latest hits, gave instruction in the new dance steps, translated Western lyrics into Polish or
Romanian, and put Hungarian or Slovak folk songs to jazz rhythms.
In the end, the regimes had to admit defeat. Hoping to recover
some influence with the youngsters, the authorities scheduled jazz
broadcasts over regime radios at hours competing with broadcasts
from the West, opened jazz clubs under the sponsorship of the Communist youth organization, and permitted the manufacture of appropriate recordings and even the importation of jazz bands from the
West.

DESTALINIZATION

After the death of Stalin on March 5, 1953, his successors undertook a basic change in policy often referred to as "destalinization."
Khrushchev initiated this policy, the substance of which was the
abandonment of police terror as a normal means of government and
the substitution of material incentives. This change meant that the
regimes had to place greater trust in their populations and to seek
to accomplish their aims primarily by persuasion and reward. The
decision to destalinize thus gave the populations a certain bargaining

power. Furthermore, destalinization meant the withdrawal of Soviet advisors and the assumption that each regime should pursue the building of Socialism in its own way. Each regime was to be autonomous. In 1955, Khrushchev attempted to achieve a reconciliation with Yugoslavia, thus bringing within the realm of the ideologically permissible the experiments which the once heretical Yugoslavs had undertaken. In 1956, the Soviet leadership was forced by the Polish upheaval to tolerate a settlement in Warsaw which included a much looser interpretation of Socialist Realism and a *modus vivendi* with the Catholic Church. The Hungarian uprising of the same year, although suppressed by Soviet military power, taught the Hungarian regime a hard lesson; once the Hungarian Communists had recovered control, they also adopted a more lenient line. Thus, destalinization meant the abandonment of terror, a generally more permissive atmosphere, and Soviet willingness to tolerate some national differences.

Neither Khrushchev nor the East European Communists intended to abandon Socialist Realism, however, or to do more than modify their other policies in the cultural field. They apparently imagined that an increased propaganda effort and occasional arrests to make clear the boundary lines of permissible action would enable them to maintain their course. However, as soon as the activity of the security police was sharply limited, under the slogan of Socialist legality, more ferment and discontent developed. One of the counter-measures adopted was a change in the educational system enacted, with some variations, in all the East European countries, including both Yugoslavia and Albania, in the years 1958-1961. One major objective of the change was to bring the younger generation under control by further increasing the polytechnical character of the educational system. To be sure, the Communist leaders also sought to increase the availability of skilled labor, but firmer control was of at least equal importance. It is part of the Communist faith that physical labor enobles, sobers, and purifies. In their language, there should be a closer tie between the schools and "life." Accordingly, the new educational system added a year of manual training distributed at various intervals along the primary and secondary educational ladder and provided certain periods (in some cases the sixth day of each week) of physical labor in factory or on farm. Students who applied for admission to the university would therefore be a year older than formerly, would know a trade, and would, presumably, have overcome the contempt for physical labor which so concerned their

superiors. Whether the educational reform of 1958-1961 much affected the basic attitudes of East European youth, however, remains
an open question.

WESTERN RADIO

The counter-forces and counter-trends which were and are indigenous were assisted significantly by developments in Western Europe
and in other areas not controlled by Communists. The astounding
economic recovery of Western Europe and the creation there of a
powerful political, economic, and cultural magnet exerted a tremendous influence throughout Eastern Europe, helped to erode
Soviet domination over intellectual life, and inexorably affected the
core of cultural life. In this situation, Western radio and tourism
and cultural exchange programs between Western and Eastern European states contributed significantly toward social and cultural
change.

The importance of Western radio in Eastern Europe is not generally understood. Western broadcasts, whether specifically directed to
the area or not, represented a major breach in the iron curtain. They
set limits on the power of the regimes to hide unpleasant truths from
their populations, and they constitute a spiritual link with the
Western world of enormous importance. The impact Western radio
has had can be measured by the enormous sums all regimes until
recently spent on jamming and by the continuing effort to attack
Western radio as irresponsible, if not meretricious.

The most important Western radio operation affecting Eastern
Europe is Radio Free Europe, an American organization with headquarters in Munich, which broadcasts in Polish, Czech, Slovak, Hungarian, Romanian, and Bulgarian and which represents approximately three-fourths of all Western broadcasts directed to the area.
Radio Free Europe serves as a substitute free press, broadcasting at
least ten minutes of news on the hour throughout the day, a considerable quantity of commentary and press review, special programs for women, youth, the intelligentsia, full coverage of Western
sporting events, and music both popular and classical.

It is clearly difficult to maintain a totalitarian system when the
regime's monopoly of news and information is constantly breached
by a substitute free press which reaches the mass of the rural populations in their own languages by short wave radio. A sample illustration is represented by the thirty-four leading Polish intellectuals who
in 1964 complained to Warsaw against increasing censorship and

other encroachments upon their freedom of thought. When the regime refused to answer the petition and began to arrest those involved, the signatories smuggled the petition and their story to the West, where there was a great outcry. When both the facts and the Western reaction reached Poland via radio, the regime surrendered and let the petitioners go free of further punishment.

TOURISM

Tourism and cultural exchange serve much the same function, opening up the closed society of totalitarianism and making possible a more normal existence. The regimes have chosen to encourage tourism because it is a relatively easy way for them to obtain the Western currencies vital for the purchase of machinery and equipment which can be obtained only in the West. However, attracting and entertaining Western tourists have created other forces which have introduced additional changes into Eastern Europe. Thus, the regimes have had to divert investment and personnel from other industries in order to build or refurbish hotels and restaurants. The improvement of transportation and of services for tourists has also affected the attitude of the regimes toward both the West and toward their own peoples with the required skills.

Furthermore, contact between Western tourists and Eastern populations has a solvent quality. Tourists visit a country only if they find the acquisition of a visa is not complicated, if the police are friendly, if the host population is gracious and lively and willing to communicate. Moreover, the impact of tourists has been and remains tremendous. East Europeans still gather around Western parked automobiles. They are astonished by the quality of the clothing worn by their visitors from the West and by their watches, cameras, and fountain pens. Above all they appreciate that the iron curtain has been breached, that they are again a part of Europe, and that all things change and will continue to change.

CULTURAL EXCHANGE

Cultural exchange is a kind of tourism at a higher and more constant level and affects the elite and the future elite of these countries. Since 1956, when it became possible for foreign scholars to do research and for artists to exhibit their talents in Eastern Europe and for American educational, scientific, and cultural institutions to invite outstanding intellectuals to the West, thousands of East Europeans have visited the West and hundreds of West Europeans and Americans have visited Eastern Europe. Programs financed and administered by individual universities, the Ford Foundation, the Inter-University Committee, the British Council, the Alliance Francaise, and the Friends Service Committee have had a profound influence on generations of intellectuals isolated for more than a decade from the rest of the world. The aims of their programs have been academic or intellectual, and they have had substantial influence on research and instruction both in the East and the West. Paradoxically, their greatest influence has been political. Even the scientist selected in part because of his Party loyalty returns a different man, with a new view of his country, himself and the world. In short, the intellectual elite, those who have traveled as well as those who have not, will never again be the same.

The Resurgence of National Cultures: 1956–1967

Beginning in 1956, the national cultures began gradually to reassert themselves, in part because of the proclamation of Khrushchev that there was no single road to Socialism, as asserted by the Stalinists, but that each people would reach the ideal society in its own way. Since 1956, diversity has become so pronounced that it is increasingly difficult to make generalizations about Eastern Europe as a whole.

Thus, Yugoslavia has developed genuine autonomy of the various constituent nations; and the quarrels and maneuverings of these six national parties have become the stuff of Yugoslav politics. In Poland, the Catholic church has reasserted something of its traditional position, and functions as a kind of government in opposition. In Czechoslovakia, Slovak nationalism has revived and exerts pressure for Slovak equality with the Czechs. On the other hand, Czech national culture has also revived, as demonstrated by the calculated recovery of Prague's primacy as a world center of the film industry; by the rehabilitation of Franz Kafka, whose works with their bitter criticism of authority and bureaucracy, were anathema to all Socialist Realists; and by the renovation of Prague itself as one of the glories of Europe. Hungarians have been visiting Vienna, ancient capital of the Austro-Hungarian monarchy, by hundreds of thousands, while Hungarian Communist leaders have stressed the traditional affinity of Hungary and Austria. The most startling case of national reassertion, however, has been provided by Romania.

ROMANIA

The period 1959–1967 has seen three related developments in Romanian culture: the rejection of Russian and Soviet sources and models; the restoration of contact with the West; and the return to national traditions.

In the 1960's, parks, streets and factories in Romania began to lose their Soviet, or even their Communist, names and revert to their pre-war nomenclature. The huge statue of Stalin which dominated central Bucharest was pulled down, and a Communist national monument containing the remains even of non-party members was erected in a major park. The building housing the Romanian-Soviet Friendship Society was closed indefinitely for repairs. The Russian language was dethroned from its place in the nation's school system, and a variety of Western languages were given equal or greater emphasis. Romanian historians began to deny that Socialism was imported from abroad and affirmed instead that it was an indigenous development with roots reaching into the nineteenth century. New party statutes, adopted in 1964, did not even mention the Great October Revolution. In 1964, the Romanian Central Committee also issued a declaration denying to the Soviet party the right to decree doctrine valid for other parties.

All jamming of Western broadcasts in the Romanian language ceased in July 1963. Because of the esoteric character of Communist politics and because of the great tensions then characterizing Soviet-Romanian relations, Bucharest could not openly appeal to its population for support in the quarrel with Moscow. However, the regime used Western radio to influence its population simply by ending jamming. About the same time, a new weekly magazine, *Lumea (The World)* by name, appeared, in format, in style, and in the use of pictures and of color, much like *Time*. Moreover, *Lumea* provides its readers with extensive, and fair-minded, excerpts from the Western press. Contemporary Western literature is also now available. At a meeting of the Writers' Union in 1964, virtually the entire corpus of that literature was granted an ideological imprimatur. Western literature was divided by the union into three classes: works which are consciously anti-capitalist such as those by Dreiser and Hemingway; works which are unconsciously anti-capitalist such as those of Rolland, Joyce, and Sartre; and works which are consciously pro-capitalist, the sole example of which was the French antinovel. A major effort to translate and publish works in the first two categories began in 1964.

This was accomplished while Romania's traditional culture was also being revived. The orthographic reform of 1952, which had sought to give the Romanian language a Slavic appearance, was abandoned. Stress was laid again on the Latin origins of Romanian and of the people who speak it. The ancient Dacians became a popular subject again, and much was written and much was taught about them. The tone of this literature was aggressive and strident. Regime policy toward minorities also changed greatly. The Saxons of Transylvania were allowed to emigrate to Germany and the Jews of Bucharest to Israel, both in small numbers but regularly. The sizeable Hungarian minority in Transylvania was subjected to forcible assimilation. In 1959, the Hungarian and Romanian universities at Cluj, the capital of the province, were merged, and thereafter Hungarian was de-emphasized as a language of instruction, both at the university and at the secondary level. In 1960, the boundaries of the Hungarian autonomous district in Transylvania were redrawn and its official title was changed to dilute its Hungarian character. More and more Romanians were appointed key officials. During the years from 1962 to 1964, furthermore, virtually every month saw the rehabilitation of some hero from the nation's past. The names are not very well known to Westerners: Titelescu in diplomacy, Iorga in history, Gusti in sociology, Octavian Goga (a member of the Fascist Iron Guard!) in poetry, and Lovinescu in drama. The plays of the exile dramatist Ionesco were performed for the first time in his native country, with Fascism identified as the target of their anti-totalitarian message. For the first time, editions of the Romanian classics have been made available on a large scale. N. Ceausescu, who succeeded Gheorghiu-Dej as party first secretary in March, 1965, addressed a meeting of writers in May and spoke of a Romanian realism, derived from the national past, which would assist the party in the building of Socialism. Socialist Realism seems to have disappeared.

The Cultural and Social Outlook

It is difficult to estimate where this will end. Had anyone predicted the Romanian national deviation in 1956, he would have been mocked, as would anyone who in 1945 had predicted the expulsion of Yugoslavia from the Cominform. Yet both of these events have taken place.

On the other hand, it appears unlikely that either Eastern Germany or Albania will be much affected by the new trends in the foreseeable future. Albania will remain a satellite because she is not only the smallest of the Communist states but also the poorest; Tirana cannot survive without a patron. Eastern Germany will remain a satellite because it rules the unhappy one-third of a nation; it cannot begin to equal by means of concessions the conditions which prevail in the happy two-thirds. If the regime should try, it might lose control. Thus, between Yugoslavia and Romania on one hand and Albania and Eastern Germany on the other, there is and will remain a great range.

Contact between Eastern Europe and the West will probably continue to increase. The jammers have now been closed, not only in Romania, but in Hungary and Poland as well; jamming of official Western broadcasts has stopped in Czechoslovakia and partially also in Bulgaria. At some point, all the populations of the area will probably acquire free access to Western broadcasts. This has meant and will mean a major improvement in the local press and radio because local media must then compete with Western radio for the attention of the population. Eastern Europe will assuredly not obtain a free press, so far as we can now foresee, but press and radio will be less dogmatic, less heavily censored, and more concerned with the interests of the public.

Tourism will continue to grow because of the rising need of the regimes for hard currencies. The growing tourist trade will add to the other pressures already working for the return to private ownership of the service industries, taxis and restaurants as well as such services as shoe repair and tailoring.

The churches may receive somewhat more freedom, as dogmatism declines and the national cultures reassert themselves. All the Eastern European Catholic hierarchies, except the Albanian, were well represented at the sessions of the Ecumenical Council. Both Prague and Budapest have recently permitted the filling of vacant sees. Belgrade concluded in 1966 a concordat with the Vatican, making Yugoslavia the first Communist state to enter an arrangement of this kind. Poland will probably be an exception to the general trend, for the percentage of believers there is very high and the influence and prestige of the hierarchy so commanding that the regime may feel compelled to continue to attack the church in order to maintain its own position. The outlook for Jewry is also favorable, partly, of course, because there are so few Jews left. The regimes already take profit in treating these remnant communities as exhibits in a museum.

Finally, it appears likely that writers and artists will gradually be vouchsafed a certain autonomy, such that on some issues the intelligentsia may recover its traditional role of critic and gadfly. Censorship and an official literary doctrine will survive, but the judicious author will be able to say most of what he thinks, so long as he expresses it in a novel or a poem. To some extent this is already true.

As part of this general grant of autonomy to the writers and the artists, university self-government and university standards will return. Class origin as a requirement for university entrance has already been dropped in most East European countries, with Bulgaria the one exception. The primacy of Russian language and literature has been overthrown in both Yugoslavia and Romania. Many universities have now reintroduced both sociology and psychiatry into their curricula. In Polish universities, courses in Marxism-Leninism were for a time abolished altogether, and the systematic study of Marxism-Leninism has no serious following.

The most striking change in the educational field has come in Czechoslovakia. Legislation adopted in 1966 in effect broke with the Soviet model of higher education and attempted to restore the situation of the universities prior to the *coup* of 1948. Rectors and deans are again to be elected by their faculties, subject to the veto of the ministry of education. Academic titles, abolished under Zhdanov, are to be restored. In academic affairs, the universities are to enjoy virtual autonomy. They will henceforth have free access to Western scientific literature. Entrance to the university is once again open only to those who have completed secondary education.

In short, massive social and cultural changes are under way in Eastern Europe. The upsurge of traditional cultural forces, the pervasive rejection of Soviet influence, and the turning to the West are all powerful factors which will continue to shape developments within and beyond the fields of social and cultural policy.

Kurt L. London

5

Eastern Europe in the Communist World

In Communist affairs, past and present are indivisible and intertwined. Historic events have a direct effect upon the present, and historic periods dovetail. Contemporary affairs cannot be understood fully without their historic antecedents; indeed, at times the past and present seem to change places. Moreover, many of us are inevitably confused because of the conspiratorial character of Communist policies and tactics. We must look at such developments as if they were a fugue, in which different lines of notes proceed independently but produce the effect of an entity when played together.

Thus, no attempt to analyze the relations of Eastern European states with Communist-ruled states elsewhere can be made without reference to history, especially that since the Second World War. Moreover, it is difficult, if not impossible, to be systematic; constant "flashbacks" are inevitable.

KURT L. LONDON *is professor of international affairs and director of the Institute for Sino-Soviet Studies, The George Washington University. He has worked on Soviet Bloc affairs in the United States Department of State and other federal agencies. Dr. London is the author of several books on Soviet affairs, Eastern Europe, and international relations.*

Background

Eastern Europe was regarded by the Czarist empire as a vital sphere of interest even before some of these states existed as national units. In the nineteenth century Russia's main contestant for influence in this area was the Austro-Hungarian empire. Germany became interested actively only after its unification in 1871, when increasing desire for expansion eastwards *(Drang nach Osten)* created misgivings both in Vienna and in St. Petersburg. After the breakup of the Hapsburg empire, the collapse of imperial Germany, and the Russian revolution, previously existing factors of stability, however precarious, no longer prevailed. In the 1930's a new situation emerged because of the rise of Stalin and Hitler, who renewed the fight for Europe's "powderkeg." This time the rationale was not only that of national security or aggrandizement, because a new powerful element made the struggle more dangerous than ever: the demand for social revolution, guided by the principles of Marx, Engels, Lenin and Stalin and backed by the Soviet Union.

The organization created in 1919 for the purpose of communist international action was the Third Communist International or Comintern. The choice of Moscow as its headquarters was inevitable, because no other country was ruled by a Communist party and because Soviet Russia, though still weak and embroiled in civil war and foreign intervention, had great potential power. Consequently, the Communist movement from the outset was dominated by Lenin's interpretation and implementation of Marxism. His philosophy and policies clearly created the political premises for the development of international communism.

There is no indication in Lenin's writings that he contemplated the domination of countries beyond the Soviet borders, and such blatant imperialism is not germane to his doctrinal teachings. He concentrated upon the development of the international communist movement and the elimination, rather than the accentuation, of nationalism. Yet, probably without weighing carefully the consequences of Soviet domination of other countries, he created the basis for Stalinist subjection of world communism to the Communist Party of the Soviet Union and of monolithic control over Eastern European countries, which became political vacua after the Teheran Conference of 1943 and the fateful Moscow Conference of 1944.

At the first of these meetings, the Western allies and the U.S.S.R.

agreed that the Soviet armies should attack Germany through Poland and the Balkans. Soviet invasion and occupation eventually led to Soviet military preponderance in Eastern Europe. The Nazi armies having been defeated and the Western allies scrupulously adhering to agreements climaxed by the Yalta Conference, overwhelming Soviet military might established itself in all the contiguous Eastern European states. Thus, Communist regimes were imposed upon these states, which became Moscow's satellites. It lay completely within Moscow's power to annex the entire territory by incorporating the individual states as "union republics." However, the Kremlin probably wanted to retain a semblance of tolerable relations with its wartime allies and may have feared that world opinion, even that of the Communist parties abroad, would react harshly. So Stalin remained content with the annexation of the Baltic states, parts of East Prussia and portions of Poland, Romania, and Czechoslovakia and with domination of the remainder of the area.

During World War II, Stalin presumably distinguished among four different categories of East European countries. First were those which had taken a stand against Nazi Germany and were contiguous to Soviet territory, Poland and Czechoslovakia. Second were Yugoslavia and Albania, non-contiguous units which had fought a guerilla war against Hitler's armies. Third were former allies of Nazi Germany—Hungary, Romania, and Bulgaria. Finally, there was the East German zone of Soviet occupation, part of former enemy territory which would become a Soviet vassal unit as the "German Democratic Republic." In spite of this diversity, the "innocence" of some states and the "guilt" of others, and despite the Yalta agreement of joint East-West responsibilities for these states, Stalin rigorously proceeded toward *Gleichschaltung* (uniformity) of the entire area under Communist tutelage.

From the very beginning, those established in positions of apparent authority in Eastern Germany have simply acted as they have been instructed. In the former "enemy countries,' Hungary, Romania and Bulgaria, "coalition" governments were set up with varying degrees of Communist participation. They were strictly transitional and soon were replaced by Communist dominated regimes and later by "people's democracies." The governments-in-exile of Poland, Czechoslovakia, and Yugoslavia eroded in various ways. In Yugoslavia, Tito and his partisans were in control at the end of the war and established a regime which through 1948 supported every Soviet policy. For a while, it seemed that Czechoslovakia would retain Masaryk's democracy, but this dream ended in 1948. Poland's emigres, instead of uniting against Moscow, fought among each other. The London Poles (the recognized Polish government-in-exile was located in London) had organized the "Home Army" to resist the Germans, but this was wiped out by the Nazis while the Soviet army refused to come to the rescue. The Western-sponsored Polish government was powerless against overwhelming Communist pressures, and soon succumbed. Albania's communist leader, Enver Hoxha, seized power without outside help as early as 1944.

It has been suggested that Stalin's interest in Eastern Europe in 1945 was still primarily strategic and economic, rather than ideological. However, by 1947, Stalin, spurred by the continuing concern of the United States for Europe, as reflected by the Truman Doctrine and the Marshall Plan, acted swiftly to impose complete ideological uniformity throughout Eastern Europe. This uniformity was characterized by total Soviet command of the local Communist Parties, massive and rapid industrialization, agricultural collectivization, and heavy emphasis on coercive state organs.

Thus, by 1948 Soviet communism had built a *cordon sanitaire*, a security belt of subject states on its western borders; had expanded the sphere of its ideological and political influence; had gained control of territories peopled by one hundred million; and had obtained areas of ready economic exploitation of raw materials, industrial production and food stuffs.

The Drive for Communist Cohesion

Although the Comintern had been dissolved by Stalin in 1943, it continued to guide the Communist parties. However, a few years later Stalin created a new international communist organization, the Communist Information Bureau or Cominform, because a communist world system was in existence and the U.S.S.R. was no longer the only communist-ruled state, and because the communist parties in many parts of the world, especially in France and Italy, had achieved strength.

THE COMINFORM

The establishment of the Cominform in 1947 should not be regarded as an attempt to revive the Comintern under a new disguise. Even though the French and Italian parties, but neither the East German nor the Albanian parties, were represented, the Cominform was designed basically to solidify Soviet control of Eastern Europe and to create a center for expounding the party line. Thus, Stalin was aware that Poland, Czechoslovakia, and Hungary were willing to negotiate Marshall Plan aid. The independent stance thus evidenced by the three states no doubt persuaded the Soviet leaders that subjection of Eastern Europe required an additional instrument to insure Soviet control and acceptance of Stalin's interpretations of Marxism-Leninism.

The rift with Yugoslavia in 1948 created a dangerous precedent, a crack in the monolithic Cominform which soon began to contribute to great and significant changes. However, with the exception of Yugoslavia, the unification and consolidation of Eastern Europe proceeded apace. The Communist revolution had become a fact, and no satellite regime could act without Stalin's nod.

Beyond the installation of Soviet control and the ideological leveling process, the Soviet dictator also sought to wipe out nationalism, using coercive and terroristic methods where necessary. Consequently, the peoples of Eastern Europe objected to communism, to the methods employed to "convert" them, and to the non-national character of the governments imposed upon them. This resentment began to fade only after 1956, when Khrushchev recognized the principle of "different roads to socialism" which had been pronounced in 1952, when Stalin was still alive, but had not been implemented.

The Cominform was the first of the instruments established to control and integrate Eastern Europe. So far as we know, it had only one plenary meeting—in 1947. All other meetings were rump conventions. Its activities consisted of policy and propaganda dissemination, chiefly through its journal, *For a Lasting Peace, For a People's Democracy!*, and through intensified communications between Moscow and the satellite capitals. Yugoslavia's defection caused considerable disquiet, but the organization carried on until 1956, the year in which polycentric communism became official policy.

However, Stalin did not consider the Cominform sufficient to ensure Soviet control. He therefore, in January 1949, established the Council for Economic Mutual Assistance, known as CEMA or COMECON, and laid the groundwork for the Warsaw Treaty Organization, established in May, 1955. Both organizations were to safeguard Soviet-East European economic and politico-military integration. CEMA was allegedly a response to the Marshall Plan.

COUNCIL FOR ECONOMIC MUTUAL ASSISTANCE

CEMA's charter members were the U.S.S.R., Poland, Czechoslovakia, Hungary, Romania, and Bulgaria. Albania, Eastern Germany and Outer Mongolia later joined; and Communist China, Yugoslavia, North Korea, and North Vietnam were invited as observers. In 1962, Mongolia was elected to regular membership, which in itself was a manifestation of the Sino-Soviet conflict; at the same time Albania ceased to attend CEMA meetings and China ceased to send observers. The task of CEMA was to achieve an integrated economic system, masterminded in Moscow. It sought to coordinate production and trade and to achieve a division of labor by assigning to the member nations specific duties on the basis of their natural resources and industrial or agricultural skills. It was clearly a restrictive system. It achieved importance when the Korean War made imperative an experimentation in economic integration to meet the need for military supplies. In fact, the satellites were prompted not only to aid in financing the war, but had to participate in the reconstruction of the North Korean economy and the industrialization of China.

THE WARSAW TREATY ORGANIZATION

The Warsaw Treaty Organization began its unofficial or "informal" career between 1948 and 1950, when numerous bilateral mutual assistance treaties were signed between the U.S.S.R. and the Eastern European states. No treaties were signed by the Soviet Union with Yugoslavia and Albania, and Eastern Germany was not admitted until 1964. At the time of its foundation, this pact was probably more a political than a military instrument. Militarily, the Soviet Union and its satellites were amply guaranteed by the bilateral agreements which they had previously signed. However, the inclusion of sovereign West Germany in the NATO system required a political response from the Kremlin. Moreover, the signing of the Austrian State Treaty on May 15, 1955, one day before the Warsaw Pact, compelled the Soviets to find a new legal excuse for the presence of Soviet troops in Eastern Europe.

Articles V and VII of the Treaty are particularly significant, for they serve as legal limitations on the sovereign powers of the Eastern European states. Article V places the armed forces of all signatories under a single command, thus far always a Soviet marshal.

Article VII prevents the signatories from entering into any other alliance, an obvious limitation of sovereignty.

The Warsaw Treaty Organization was therefore in its early days considered a kind of political holding corporation designed to foster a consensual outlook on foreign policy, and to encourage uniformity on social and governmental levels. Its military importance has grown since the early sixties, despite (or perhaps as a result of) the spread of polycentrism. Thus, with its gradual and partial demise as an instrument of Soviet political domination, its significance as a military alliance directed against any West German threat has apparently become increasingly important to the so-called "northern tier"— Poland, Czechoslovakia, and Eastern Germany. Romania, as in the economic field, has manifested an unusual degree of independence by its reluctance to form a close military attachment. The significance of the Romanian position should not be overemphasized, because the recognized power and policy of the Soviet Union severely limit Romania's freedom of action. It is difficult to believe that the Soviet Union, even in a polycentric era, would allow any of its Eastern European "allies" to leave a military organization which involves Soviet security and Moscow's already weakened political position in a vital sphere of interest. Moreover, the very strength of the Soviet-East European military alliance guarantees the position of the Soviet Union and its allies in any negotiations with NATO.

When Stalin died in 1953, the Cominform then was no more than a weekly journal, published in many languages; CEMA was still seeking its bearings; the Warsaw Treaty Organization was just an accumulation of bilateral defense treaties between the U.S.S.R. and its vassal states. Yet the old dictator, through the very presence of his powerful personality, had achieved monolithic control from which only Yugoslavia escaped. There is evidence, however, that some doubts had entered the minds of Stalin and some of his lieutenants concerning the permanence of such a system of controls. Some phraseology in Malenkov's report at the Nineteenth Congress of the Soviet Communist Party in 1952 reveals some uneasiness and a need to reassure the satellites that Soviet relations with the East European and Asian communist states would be based on "the principles of equality, economic cooperation and respect for national independence." Malenkov then spoke for Stalin; as Stalin's successor, he did not noticeably modify Stalinist policies in Eastern Europe. It was only when Khrushchev took over that more radical changes occurred than the Soviet leadership could have anticipated.

The Emergence of Polycentrism

In February 1956, at the Twentieth Congress of the Soviet Communist Party, Khrushchev destroyed Stalin's image and thereby, unwittingly, the vanguard position of world communism's leading party. Furthermore, he elevated to a Soviet doctrine the concept of "different roads to socialism," or national adaptations of Marxism-Leninism to the specific conditions of individual countries. Coercive measures were replaced by voluntaristic ones. Khrushchev apparently believed that common ideological bonds were strong enough to permit more flexibility to the Eastern European states, provided they traveled the road to communism under the over-all guidance of Moscow. This assumption was reinforced by the thesis that, because of the strength of the "socialist camp," war was no longer inevitable and that communist ends could be achieved through parliamentary means, that is, by a sequence of infiltration, evolution and bloodless revolution when the evolutionary stage had prepared the way for the final push.

The year 1956 was crucial for international communism. The Party Congress and the denigration of Stalin threw the movement into confusion; the Cominform was abolished; revolt in Poland and revolution in Hungary upset Eastern Europe; the October 30th declaration of the Soviet government "on the principles of development and further strengthening of friendship and cooperation between the Soviet Union and other socialist states" sought to confirm and codify the character of this new relationship; Yugoslavia's independence, after the Khrushchev-Bulganin pilgrimage to Belgrade in 1955, was enhanced; Togliatti in Italy popularized the term polycentrism, to which he pledged allegiance; and, in 1957, Mao experimented with the "hundred flower" episode, which was intended as a slight concession to China's intellectuals and became a violent denunciation of the regime. Instead of one center's dominating the international movement, many flowered throughout the "socialist camp." Communist parties outside the orbit began to adopt a more independent stance. The Chinese communists, who apparently had not been consulted by the Kremlin, seemed to accept the new positions, but we know now that they resented having been confronted with a *fait accompli* and fundamentally disagreed. Still, they continued until 1960 to proclaim the Soviet Party the leading party.

In Eastern Europe, de-Stalinization caused such convulsions that

Chou En-lai, after the Polish outbreaks and the Hungarian revolution, flew to Warsaw, Budapest, and Moscow as a mediator. The Mao regime clearly feared further disintegration of the "socialist camp"; it was concerned lest a fractionalization of Communist parties in Europe affect its own party's position. As seen from Peking, the Soviet Union and Eastern Europe after 1956 were tainted with revisionism. However, Communist parties remained in power; one must remember this when speculating on the extent of the former satellites' new "independence."

While there was a trend toward moderation after the end of the Stalin era, this was not the case in Albania. The conflict between the Stalinist leaders of Tirana and the de-Stalinized leadership in Moscow and in Belgrade had its origins in World War II and has so many ramifications that it is not possible to recount them within the framework of this chapter. Albania's Communists had tolerated Yugoslav exploitation and territorial designs so long as they occurred under Stalinist auspices. The Hoxha regime became firmly entrenched in Albania after Yugoslavia's break with Stalin, when Tirana's enmity against heretic Belgrade became boundless. When the U.S.S.R. in 1955 sought reconciliation with Yugoslavia, Albanian hostility toward Belgrade encompassed Moscow as well.

The events of 1956 were as displeasing to Tirana as they were to Peking. Indeed, Albania was less cautious in showing its bad temper than was China, which seven years later made it clear that the 1956 Soviet Party Congress was the source of the disagreements. As the tension between Moscow and Peking grew and became public knowledge, it is not surprising that Albania sought and found a close alliance with China. Of all Eastern European states, Albania alone has rejected polycentrism as "modern revisionism" and has remained strictly dogmatist.

In short, at the end of 1956, Eastern European communism was a shambles, and the Kremlin was compelled to take steps to prevent further deterioration. Prior to the November 1957 communist summit, it convoked innumerable meetings, bilateral and multilateral, for representatives of parties and governments. This extraordinary diplomatic feat succeeded, and stability had been restored by November 1957. However, polycentrism had not been abandoned. The statement issued by the 1957 communist summit conference in Moscow was as Bolshevik a document as ever promulgated and was signed by the Chinese. However, it failed to restore the monolith; Chinese attempts to create a new world-wide organization, another Comintern, had as little success as similar later attempts by Khrushchev. However, during the period since 1957 both CEMA and the Warsaw Treaty Organization have been rejuvenated as pragmatic implementations of the "socialist commonwealth."

The Socialist Commonwealth

During the years 1955–1960, the organization of the "socialist camp" was the principal problem facing the communist leaders. The Comintern could not be revived. The development of polycentric communism which had enabled the East European states to free themselves, up to a point, from Soviet domination at least in *internal* affairs caused them to fear that any new organization would fall under Moscow's sway. Parties outside the communist orbit eagerly seized the idea of polycentrism and the changed relationship between Eastern Europe and the Soviet Union as a model for the transition from vassalage to simple deference to the power and experience of the Soviet regime. Since, therefore, a new organization would be opposed by East European leaders, with the possible exception of Eastern Germany and, temporarily, Czechoslovakia and Bulgaria, Khrushchev developed the ingenious idea of a "commonwealth of socialist countries," an organization without organization, a voluntaristic, loose association of states with kindred beliefs and common hatreds.

The "socialist commonwealth" began very slowly. On the other hand, governmental legal and social concepts of the U.S.S.R. were applied in the Eastern European states, thus preparing the degree of consensus which was necessary in the late fifties when the commonwealth idea was enhanced through a series of treaties such as the Dual-Nationality and Consular Conventions. Agreements on unification of legal systems and cultural exchange programs were also concluded during these years. In the economic sphere, seventeen bilateral treaties on commerce and navigation were signed between 1949 and 1960 by the members of the commonwealth, i.e. by practically all communist-ruled nations.

The "socialist commonwealth" was to be world-wide. It was open to any state which decided to join the socialist camp. It had no conditions, such as those which had limited membership to the Comintern, and the difference between the rigid doctrinal position of that revolutionary body and the rather casual concept of the "commonwealth" demonstrates clearly the great change in approach to organization.

Several steps were taken to implement and strengthen the association design. In March 1956, a Joint Institute for Nuclear Research was founded in the Soviet Union at Dubna, with twelve states, including Eastern Germany and North Vietnam, by the end of the year. The costs were determined according to the members' financial capabilities, with the U.S.S.R. paying almost half and Communist China about twenty per cent. In 1956, a Railway Cooperation Organization was established at Sofia, Bulgaria, to coordinate transportation, tariffs, frontier facilities, and even automotive problems. In 1957, a Communications Cooperation Organization was established for technical and economic coordination. This organization has no governing body, but it holds an annual meeting.

Perhaps even more important, between 1955 and 1959 a number of friendship and cooperation treaties were signed. China and Eastern Germany were first in 1955, followed by agreements between China and Czechoslovakia and Mongolia and Czechoslovakia in 1957, and China and Hungary in 1959. In 1958, the Political Consultative Committee of the Warsaw Treaty Organization met. The member states were represented by their highest ranking governmental leaders, and Communist China was among the observers. The meeting was apparently an attempt to devise an integrated Warsaw Pact-Asian defense system for the creation of peace zones in European and Pacific areas, but these plans collapsed because of the growing Sino-Soviet dispute. There was a lively exchange of visits by Europeans in East and Southeast Asia. Ho Chi Minh visited Eastern Europe in 1957, and the then Chinese Defense Minister Peng Te-huai led a military delegation to the U.S.S.R. and Eastern Europe in 1959.

However, with all the "traditional" and legal aspects binding the commonwealth, the political element was decisive. This explains why the concept has suffered a great setback since the quarrel between Moscow and Peking became public. In 1959, a leading Soviet jurist declared that "the socialist countries are states which are led and directed by the Communist and Workers' parties. It naturally and necessarily follows, therefore, that the inspirers and organizers of the new stage in the progressive movement of mankind, and particularly in international relations and international law, are the Communist parties . . ." The vanguard of these parties remained, the jurist claimed, the Soviet Party. This claim was accepted by the eighty-one parties which met at the Moscow conference in 1960. Two years later, in another meeting of the Communist and Workers Parties, which may be looked upon as the curators of the commonwealth, it was declared that

> the commonwealth of socialist countries realizes its goals through comprehensive political, economic and cultural cooperation. In this, all socialist countries are strictly guided by the principles of full equality, mutual respect for independence and sovereignty, fraternal mutual aid and mutual advantage. In the socialist camp, no one has or can have any special rights or privileges. The observance of the principles of Marxism-Leninism and socialist internationalism is an indispensable condition for the successful development of the world socialist system.

By that time, however, these high-sounding phrases had become mere verbiage.

Divisive Issues

The Sino-Soviet conflict has changed the character and dimmed the chances of the "commonwealth" and made unrealizable its declared principles. Following the first public Chinese Communist outburst in April, 1960, the "socialist camp" has become bi-polar. North Korea and North Vietnam apparently leaned toward Peking, while Eastern Europe, with the exception of Albania, has rallied to Moscow in various degrees of intensity. Romania alone has tried to stay "neutral."

Gita Ionescu of the University of London suggests three interlocking issues which divide the camp into dogmatists (in the Soviet view, Communist China), and revisionists (in the Chinese Communist view, the U.S.S.R.) These issues are, first, leadership and solidarity of the communist movement; second, communist strategy for the achievement of eventual victory; and third, the differing economic standards between communist states. The first two are particularly crucial in the relations of Eastern Europe with the communist world.

The question of leadership has become a primary consideration since the Peking-Moscow quarrel erupted publicly. In Eastern Europe, it began with the arrival of polycentrism in 1956 within the regional context. It was known, however, that the Chinese Communist leaders were opposed to polycentrism, because they were convinced that communism requires central direction. Even as late as 1959, the Chinese Communists were willing to concede the "vanguard" position to Moscow. Peking's desire for international proletarian solidarity suffered a decisive setback when Moscow reneged on its promise to assist in building nuclear facilities and when the Soviet leaders withdrew their technical personnel, depriving China of badly needed help in industrialization. These Soviet sanctions raised once again the issue of the uneven material-technical development of the countries of the socialist camp, which was of concern also to Eastern European states and was expressed most strongly by Romania.

There are thus two main factors undermining Peking's desire for communist cohesion on its terms: East European polycentrism, and Sino-Soviet rivalry for leadership of the movement and for predominance in the so-called third world. The former did not disturb Peking prior to the outbreak of its quarrel with Moscow. Indeed, after Chou En-lai returned from his visit to Eastern Europe in January 1957, Peking joined Moscow in supporting the independence and equality of socialist states.

The Yugoslav direction toward "national communism" led to very severe attacks by China against the Tito regime, more than Moscow was inclined to condone. Tito's example almost certainly changed the outlook of the Chinese Communists toward polycentrist Eastern Europe, which reached a climax at the Bucharest and Moscow conferences in 1960, when Albania left the Soviet bloc to join China. Whatever regrets some East European communists may have had that their relations with China had deteriorated were later dispersed by the extraordinary confusion of Mao's "great proletarian cultural revolution." Indeed, China's political isolation following its foreign policy failures in Africa and Asia, especially Indonesia, and its "permanent revolution" have done much to restore communist loyalties to the Soviet line.

The issue of communist strategy is basically a question of interpretation of the Marxist-Leninist doctrine in political, economic, and military terms. Interpretations have changed as a result of communist postwar ideological and territorial advances, which resulted in the development of the "socialist camp" and the growth of communist parties all over the world. When the Chinese communists took control of the mainland, more than a billion human beings were then under Communist rule. At the same time, the colonial empires began to crumble, more or less peacefully, and the "semi-colonial" countries attained sovereignty: a "third world" was born. Finally, the achievements of Soviet technology in nuclear and outer space fields led to disagreement concerning strategy between Moscow and Peking. Severe differences of opinion developed and became evident concerning all of these issues. Soviet thought on these subjects has not been accepted by the Chinese leaders.

The Eastern European states in this debate have supported the Soviet point of view, not only because they had no choice but also because they rejected the Chinese view of "peaceful coexistence" as a brief tactical ruse, Chinese insistence on a belligerent "national liberation war," and Chinese reckless disdain for the consequences of nuclear attack. Therefore, Eastern Europe has accepted the Kremlin's conversion of "peaceful coexistence" from a tactical device under Stalin to its present strategic position.

The problem of different economic levels in the component states of the "camp" is less important in Eastern Europe than in China. Indeed, the living standard in some of the former satellites has improved significantly since 1956. For example, Eastern Germany is now the tenth country in the world in industrial production. Great economic advances have been made in Romania, Hungary, and, to some extent, Poland and Czechoslovakia. Despite the agricultural problems the Eastern European countries face, their economies maintain satisfactory growth rates. Thus, the question of uneven development on the road to socialism is not a vital one so far as Eastern European relations with other communist countries are concerned, although it is an issue that concerns the U.S.S.R. and Communist China and has contributed to the deep misunderstanding between the two countries.

A brief summary of the impact of the Sino-Soviet conflict on Eastern Europe reveals that the Chinese as late as 1957 still collaborated with the Soviets to restore unity of the movement. Mao then spoke of world communism "headed by the Communist Party of the Soviet Union." Chinese cooperation, however, was greatly impaired by Soviet and Eastern European reactions to the establishment of the Peoples' Communes and the "Great Leap Forward," when the Mao regime committed the heresy of seeking to skip the stage of socialism in order to proceed directly to communism.* This reckless venture,

---

* According to Marxism-Leninism, socialism is the first, lower phase of a communist revolution whose task it is to liquidate capitalism and replace it with a socio-economic system that features state (or community) rather than private property. Goods are distributed according to the principle: "to each what he deserves." During this phase, social classes gradually will be eliminated and a material-technical base established for the "transition to communism." When class differences no longer exist and the state "withers away," the second, higher phase of the revolution will be initiated in which citizens "receive what they need": communism. Communists believe it is possible to skip historic stages of

which failed, contributed to mutual ill feeling. The Khrushchev trip to the United States in 1959 and the ensuing "spirit of Camp David" added to dissension. Khrushchev's subsequent visit to Peking was a failure, and the Chinese leader who apparently advocated Sino-Soviet rapprochement, Defense Minister Marshal Peng Te-huai, was purged.

When the Sino-Indian conflict began smoldering in 1959, the Chinese position was not supported by the Kremlin, leading the Chinese communists to complain that never in the history of the "socialist camp" had a socialist state taken a neutral position vis-à-vis another. In that same year, the twenty-first congress of the Soviet Party took place under the sign of a détente between the U.S.S.R. and the United States: it emphasized the policy or strategy of peaceful coexistence, it proposed a nuclear test ban, and it suggested normalization of relations with the United States. This infuriated the Chinese, but pleased the Eastern European nations, who began to watch Peking's aggressive policies with apprehension.

These events inevitably led to the exacerbation of the conflict at the twenty-second congress of the Soviet party in 1961. Albania then was the only Eastern European state which in defiance of the Soviet Union joined China and was promptly excommunicated by Moscow. Perhaps because Albania and China continued to venerate Stalin, another attack on the former leader of world communism at that congress widened the chasm. It also stimulated polycentric de-Stalinization in those Eastern European states which had not until then made much progress in ridding themselves of the symbols and the content of Stalinism.

The Kremlin, then under Khrushchev's rule, tried to exert pressure on the Asian communist regimes and parties by economic measures and defense treaties. However, Khrushchev's plan to reinvigorate CEMA failed. Trade between the Eastern European states deteriorated, as did party relations. Plans for a consolidated master plan of economic integration through CEMA were obstructed by Romania, which since 1963 has refused to take part in the great division of labor the Kremlin had sought. Worse still, Soviet attempts to convoke a conference to complete the isolation of Communist China have failed. Even after the dismissal of Khrushchev in October 1964,

---

social development prior to the socialist phase (e.g. in the underdeveloped countries), but that communism cannot be achieved until the way has been prepared by socialism. (Logically, while "socialism in one country" is feasible, a communist island cannot exist in a sea of non-communist societies. It follows that without a world-wide victory of the revolution, communism is unattainable.)

his successors have followed the same unsuccessful policy of attempting to convoke such a conference.

The elimination of Khrushchev was not popular in Eastern Europe. Contrary to their pious protestations for communist unity, Eastern European leaders probably were apprehensive that the heirs to Khrushchev would succeed in achieving a rapprochement with the Mao regime. The Sino-Soviet conflict had forced the Kremlin into greater permissiveness toward its former satellites, and Eastern Europeans recognized that an end of the conflict could bring about new personnel and organizational arrangements. To be sure, Romania sent a delegation to Peking and negotiated with Chou En-lai, but without success. This action probably was more a symbol of Romania's newly proclaimed sovereignty than a maneuver designed to mediate. Besides, Bucharest must have discussed its plan with Moscow and obtained permission for that venture. In any event, the U.S.S.R. has made a strong bid for a comeback in Asia; as the situation in mainland China has worsened and as the war in Vietnam has escalated, it has succeeded to a certain degree. China's earlier impact had been blunted by the American presence in Southeast Asia; the breakdown of communism in Indonesia deprived it of opportunities, and the quickly rising prosperity in some countries of East and Southeast Asia had condemned it to play second fiddle.

Meanwhile, the Eastern European states signed aid agreements with North Vietnam in 1965, and delegations from Moscow and Budapest visited North Korea and Vietnam to strengthen the cohesion of the camp in Asia. However, no political agreement seems to have been reached. Czechoslovak, Hungarian, Bulgarian, and Polish delegates concurred with Moscow's policy of socialist unification in Asia. The commonwealth idea had not entirely died.

The 1960's

By far the most important relations Eastern European states maintain are those with the Soviet Union. When we speak of international relations, we mean free interplay between sovereign states. While Stalin was alive, this term could not be applied to the satellite states, which were actually ruled by the Kremlin, directly or by proxy. Conditions for relations began to develop, albeit on a somewhat restricted scale, only after 1956, when a greater degree of internal freedom of movement and of economic development became permissible and when slow progress toward sovereignty began. However, such is not the case in matters of foreign policy and military strategy. Romania's attempts to trade with the West and the conclusion of political treaties are quite separate matters. Resistance against CEMA planning may be viewed by Moscow as a matter to be settled "internally," i.e. among bloc nations, but deserting the Warsaw Pact would affect Soviet defense policy and cannot be even considered. Romania has curtailed the number of its army conscripts, but it still must contribute to the Warsaw Treaty Organization and its services must remain within the general framework of the Pact's provisions.

POLAND

Poland's close relations with the Soviet Union are based heavily on its fear of Germany. There is no peace treaty; the Oder-Neisse line officially is a border unilaterally determined by the East but not recognized by the West. After the forcible expulsion of Germans from their territory, partially the result of Soviet annexation of Eastern Polish land, the former German area has become the agricultural and industrial mainstay of the Polish economy and, at the same time, a constant source of fear of future German action. The Poles therefore must rely on Soviet support, and their foreign and military policies parallel those of the U.S.S.R. Internally, their regime is communist but Polish, and is regarded as such by the population.

EASTERN GERMANY

Eastern Germany has made strong economic advances to which the monstrous Berlin Wall has contributed by keeping potential refugees inside and impressing on the population the futility of further opposition. Eastern Germany is the heartland of former Prussia, and the Prussian view of duty as the essence of existence, and the inborn respect for *Obrigkeit* (authority) have combined to channel despair into resignation and productive work. The "German Democratic Republic" has been the most active of all the Eastern European States in trying to establish relations with non-European states, but it is still the most subordinate state in the Soviet security belt and has remained a satellite. It is economically exploited by Moscow and has little voice in world affairs. Contiguous to Soviet territory and occupied by some twenty divisions of the Soviet army, allegedly to safeguard communications, it remains chained to Moscow.

HUNGARY

Relations between Hungary and the U.S.S.R. are now excellent. Kadar, who pulled Hungary out of the despair and ruin of 1956, appears to have the confidence of the present Kremlin leaders, just as he had that of Khrushchev. Since the early sixties, he has succeeded in obtaining understanding and support from the Hungarian people, who know that he was installed by the Soviet army and who had considered him a Soviet puppet, but who have been affected by the relaxation of restrictions and by the considerable improvement in living conditions. However, the basic communist policies have not changed, and Soviet dominance in foreign and military affairs has remained paramount.

CZECHOSLOVAKIA

In Czechoslovakia, the Stalinist terror of the first five years after the coup in 1948 did not abate after the dictator's death, and progress toward more relaxation was slow even after 1956. Novotný's policy was crowned with the proclamation in 1960 of Czechoslovakia as the second socialist country. Since that time, the economy has stagnated, the intelligentsia have demanded reforms, and the old quarrels between Czechs and Slovaks have worsened. When Khrushchev was dismissed, Novotný objected, and there was tension between Moscow and Prague until late in 1964. Czechoslovakia fears Germany, though not to the extent Poland does. Its territorial gains at the end of the war were minor, but the expulsion of the German Sudeten minority has naturally increased Czech fears of ultimate German demands. However should West Germany officially abrogate the Munich agreements of 1938, diplomatic relations between Czechoslovakia and the Federal Republic of Germany might be resumed.

Thus, Czechoslovakia still depends on its eastern neighbor. It cooperates with Soviet political and economic policy and has become well integrated in the Warsaw Treaty Organization in its military maneuvers. It has acted for Moscow in providing arms to areas of revolutionary import in Africa and Asia. Even the changes since the late fifties have not removed it far from satellite status.

BULGARIA

Even more than Czechoslovakia, Bulgaria has remained a satellite of its Slav brother. It has acted as the Kremlin's proxy in the matter of communist conference organization; it did not object to Khrushchev's dismissal. The visit of its Foreign Minister to Paris and its consideration of the establishment of diplomatic relations with Bonn were almost certainly sanctioned and perhaps initiated by Moscow.

ROMANIA

Romania is different, and since 1963 has had more independence than any other former satellite. The Romanian leaders have tried to profit from the Sino-Soviet conflict, and Romania's April 1964 statement concerning relations with other communist countries has been called the "Romanian Declaration of Independence." This document opposed all centralized planning within the "socialist camp" and rejected interference by one party in the affairs of another. It put Romania on the Soviet side in the conflict with Red China but also reproached the Kremlin for its part in the quarrel. Romania supports an international communist conference, but its condition that all parties participate destroys any possibility for a conference because the Chinese and Albanian Parties will not attend. Romania has continued to try to mediate the Sino-Soviet conflict. Since the Bucharest leaders must have realized that their attempts would not succeed, their trips to Peking presumably were made to demonstrate their independence of action.

Similar independent actions have been undertaken in the economic area. Romania has opposed the Soviet attempt to use CEMA as an instrument for economic integration. It has also made separate economic agreements with Western states, particularly France. However, it can hardly act against the Kremlin's foreign policy or military strategy. It remains, perforce, part of the Soviet security area and cannot stretch the limits of its own policies beyond the barriers the Kremlin has erected. Its policies toward France have coincided with Soviet trends toward Soviet-French accommodation. Similarly, the agreement between Romania and West Germany to establish full diplomatic relations, a step which must be regarded as primarily economic, must be understood and accepted as such by the Soviet Union.

ALBANIA

The Albanian break with the U.S.S.R., but not with all Eastern European states, has continued since 1961. Since Albania is so isolated and has such meager resources, the Soviet Union is surely not disturbed by the Albanian affiliation with Communist China. Moreover, Albania has little impact within Eastern Europe. For Moscow, Albania's most important function was that it served for a while as a target for attacks directed against China. Its present position has saved the U.S.S.R., Eastern Germany and Czechoslovakia the expenditures for aid, which now is provided by Communist China.

YUGOSLAVIA

Yugoslavia is an independent state controlled by Communists whose political complexion is a strange mixture of pragmatic Leninism, evolutionary socialism, multi-faceted nationalism, and cosmopolitan aspirations. Tito's relations with the U.S.S.R. have oscillated since 1955. As the changes since 1956 have produced an increasing trend toward polycentrism and concomitantly a greater degree of freedom of movement under regimes headed by national leaders rather than Soviet proxies, Yugoslav resistance against Moscow's central control and its revisionist reforms has lost something of its luster. Tito has never concealed his predilection for the East, and his dealings with the West, especially the United States, have been prompted by pure opportunism.

Yugoslavia's relations with Albania and China are similar to those between the U.S.S.R. and these two countries. One might assume that the Sino-Soviet conflict supports Tito's position vis-à-vis the other Communist states. His foreign and military policies are not bound by those of Moscow. However his attempts to gain influence in the third world by posing as an "uncommitted" nation have had little success. Tensions in Asia and détente in Europe are helpful to him, and his denunciation of the American presence in Vietnam is not convincing.

Little can be said about Eastern European relations with Communist parties in noncommunist countries. The diplomatic offices are in charge of maintaining such relations, and practically nothing is known about the nature of these contacts. None of these states appears to foster aggressive revolutionary designs, none is in a position to contribute financially to the coffers of foreign parties, and the Soviet Union itself almost certainly controls all such contacts, so Eastern Europe's role here is probably not important. Eastern European agents have been identified in a number of cases of espionage, but it is not clear whether they worked on behalf of their own country or for the Soviet Union. One could speculate that agents from Eastern Europe are being used by Moscow, whenever feasible, and there no doubt is close cooperation between the Soviet and Eastern European secret services. Coordination of these services and of other activities is suggested by the arrest late in 1966 of a naturalized (former Czech) U.S. citizen by Czechoslovak agents in a Soviet plane on the way from Moscow to Paris during a nonscheduled landing in Prague under an obviously artificial pretext. It also proves that the nationalism of Eastern European governments is tainted and modified by the Marxist-Leninist base on which they operate.

Some Conclusions

During the past decade, great changes have occurred in the nature of Eastern European relations with other communist-ruled countries. The leveling process which Stalinist communism imposed upon the states of this area and which did not cease even after Yugoslavia's ejection from the Cominform in 1948, slowed after Stalin's death and has petered out since 1956. However, the governing parties of these states remain dedicated to Marxism-Leninism, even though they have modified it to suit their individual purposes in accordance with the thesis that each country may proceed toward socialism along its national road.

There is a strong determination to restore sovereignty. Selected components of nationalism, long repressed, have appeared again, but there is a contradiction between the communist (international) ideology and the more limited aims of nationalism. If communism still is considered a motivating power in the Soviet bloc, then "national communism" is a paradox and "communism in one country" an impossible proposition: it is no longer Marxism-Leninism.

Furthermore, Eastern Europe is not an entity, but a diversified region in which each state has its own history, needs, and aspirations. All these states have undergone the torture of enforced communist uniformity. Even though they have shed some of the consequences of Stalinization, their parties and governments are still affected by it. Beyond this ideological impact, which has been modified in the wake of polycentrism, are the hard facts of overwhelming Soviet power, Soviet contiguity, and Moscow's political, economic and strategic goals. Even if ideological deviation no longer is a ground for Soviet sanctions, even if internal politics no longer are subject to corrective coercion by the Soviet Party, Eastern Europe is still regarded by the Kremlin as a vital security sphere. Should deviations become so powerful as to endanger the Soviet position in circumstances in which Moscow could act, the Soviet Union would almost certainly seek to check the deterioration. It has important weapons it can use.

The economies of Eastern Europe remain predominantly directed

toward the U.S.S.R., and Western efforts to build bridges and to
strengthen economic ties between East and West face serious difficulties. The Eastern European states clearly welcome increased economic
ties with Western Europe. The Soviet Union has thus far refrained
from interfering and will no doubt continue this policy so long as
the increased ties continue to benefit both the Soviet Union and
Eastern Europe and do not significantly affect the Soviet Union's
position in Eastern Europe. Since about two thirds of Eastern European trade is confined to the Soviet area, it cannot be excluded that
the countries of the security belt are in fact acting as proxies for the
U.S.S.R. It is conceivable, but hardly likely, that CEMA, Romania
notwithstanding, could become a center from which the type and
nature of trade with the West would be determined by both Moscow
and its Eastern European allies.

Militarily, the Warsaw Treaty Organization has developed into a
body encompassing well-trained and reliable units, particularly from
countries whose strategic importance requires priority consideration,
Poland, Czechoslovakia, and Hungary. Although there is some pressure for a rotating command, Soviet marshals have remained in
charge and in control. In a similar vein, Eastern European diplomats, dominated by the Party Politbureaus, could hardly pursue a
policy which was in any way opposed to Soviet policy. Sensational as
Romania's antics may appear, even her claim for sovereignty has
limits. Western observers should not ignore the hard fact that the
Soviet leaders, present and future, are not likely to permit polycentrism to spread to such an extent that it would cause a new
balkanization of Eastern Europe.

The basic change that has occurred since 1956 is that the Eastern
European states are permitted to have international relations with
many countries. Under Stalin, such relations did not exist, for all
satellite parties and governments were merely handmaidens of the
Kremlin dictator. Now they can talk back. Their relations with other
countries are freer. Nevertheless, they remain in the socialist brother-
hood of the commonwealth, and the lion's share in the international
affairs of Eastern Europe belongs to Moscow.

This greater freedom of movement by East European governments
has had the effect of strengthening the polycentric philosophy of
communist parties outside the "socialist camp." For example, both
the Italian and French parties have been encouraged, and Moscow's
permissiveness has supported the repeated Soviet claim that all
socialist states are sovereign and equal. This permissiveness has also

encouraged a broader political outlook by smaller Communist parties. Thus, the Danish Communist Party has moved toward the center of the Danish political spectrum and now plays a uniquely active role for a Communist party in Scandinavia.

A very important by-product of Eastern European polycentrism can be noted in Western foreign policies. General de Gaulle and other West European leaders have initiated economic and cultural cooperation with the Eastern European states. The United States has proclaimed a desire to "build bridges" to the area. These policies undoubtedly strengthened the West German government's decision to loosen its Hallstein Doctrine, which constrained Bonn from maintaining relations with states having diplomatic representations in East Germany, and to establish diplomatic relations with Romania.

It is impossible to predict whether the changing Western attitude will succeed in strengthening East European independence, or whether, in the long run, it will merely fortify Communist control of the area under Soviet power. Until there is demonstrable proof one way or the other, we must not permit the recent progress toward greater Eastern European independence from Moscow to obscure our analyses.

John C. Campbell

6

Europe, East and West

Following the Second World War, there were in fact two Europes, East and West, kept apart by the political and ideological rigidities of the cold war and by their association, respectively, with hostile alliance systems led by two essentially non-European great powers. The Soviet Union, while not limiting its aims, was determined to keep the positions it had won by the advance of the Soviet army into the heart of Europe in the closing stages of the war, although it later accepted Yugoslavia's defection and the independence of a neutral Austria. Neither the United States nor the nations of Western Europe regarded this division of the continent as compatible with their long-term aims for a soundly-based European settlement. They did not feel at all comfortable with Soviet forces encamped on the Elbe. So long as no settlement was in sight, however, the generally agreed policy was to work for greater strength and unity in the West and to hold firm against threats, while refraining from any attempt to challenge the Soviet position in Eastern Europe by force and while keeping open the channels of negotiation with Moscow.

A settlement is still not in sight. However, the familiar political

---

JOHN C. CAMPBELL, *Senior Research Fellow of the Council on Foreign Relations, was formerly deputy director of the Office of East European Affairs and a member of the Policy Planning Staff of the U. S. Department of State. He has served as political advisor to the government and as consultant to many institutions interested in Eastern Europe. Dr. Campbell is the author of many books and articles on international affairs.*

landscape of the postwar period has been changing, since 1956 in particular. Trends within each of the two blocs, and between them, have introduced a state of movement opening up new vistas to governments and peoples on both sides of the now somewhat rusty and porous iron curtain. There is much talk of bringing the two Europes together in some kind of new unity. "Europe from the Atlantic to the Urals" is the professed aim of General de Gaulle. "Europe for the Europeans," says the voice of Moscow, meaning a Europe from which American influence is excluded. The same words come from the East European capitals, but not always with the same meaning. "Building bridges to Eastern Europe" and "peaceful engagement" are Washington's contributions to the rash of slogans and declarations dedicated to the general goal of ending the partition of the continent. Slogans are not policies, and there are hard elements of national interest and of global military strategy which continue to affect the attitudes and actions of the two principal powers on each side. Yet there is no doubt that the Europeans themselves will have more to say about their own destiny than they have had since 1945. Nor can Eastern Europe's future any longer be considered apart from that of Western Europe.

Before attempting to discuss the practical questions involved in relations between the two Europes—more accurately, between the various individual states on both sides—it is well to look into history and to examine some of the underlying attitudes which bear, positively or negatively, on the future relations between the two halves of the continent. One question has to do with the reality of the sense of European community on both sides. If a revived nationalism is strong enough to break down the existing blocs, will it not also be a barrier to the creation of a new and wider European unity? A second question is whether the nations of the area we know today as Eastern Europe have ever been an integral part of the historic European community.

As Stephen Kertesz points out in his introductory chapter, Eastern Europe through the ages has been a fringe area, a borderland without unity of its own. Many of its nations have been set apart from the West by differences in political experience, economic development, civilization, and culture. It is sufficient to cite the continuing struggle of German and Slav in the "eastern marchlands," the religious split between Roman Catholic and Eastern Orthodox, and the profound differences between those who endured centuries of Turkish rule and those who escaped it. The old question of where the "East" begins never received the same answer from the various nations inhabiting the geographic area known as Europe. Some of the attitudes and prejudices stemming from history persist in contemporary international politics. They help to explain why some thought it natural to go forward with the building of European unity in the West without regard to the nations of the East, not merely because the latter were prevented from joining by the power of Russia but because they did not really belong anyway.

On the other hand, history shows many links as well as differences. Some of the nations in our presently defined Eastern Europe, such as Poland, Czechoslovakia, and Hungary, were historically part of central Europe, connected with the West through political association and the influence of Catholicism. Even in the Balkans, the natural ties with Russia through Slavdom and Orthodoxy have had to compete with the ideas of the French Revolution and of German Romanticism, which inspired the leaders of the national renascence of the Christian peoples in the nineteenth century. In Russia itself, this same question of where the nation's destiny lay, in Europe or outside it, was posed both in intellectual debate and in governmental policy.

The First World War saw the triumph of the Western democracies, with which the cause of national self-determination in Eastern Europe was linked. For a brief period, the East European nations were very much a part of European politics, although divided among themselves and caught in the toils of great-power conflicts. The establishment of Communist power in Russia was a challenge to all of Europe, but the rise of Fascism and National Socialism in Italy and Germany rejected the spirit of the West and broke its unity. Who would claim that the Germans under Hitler were better representatives of Western European civilization than the peoples whom they overran and enslaved? Caught between great powers and great ideological forces, the East European nations saw their independence destroyed. Encroachments both from the German and the Russian side marked the period between 1938 and 1941. Then came four years of Nazi domination, followed by the imposition of Soviet domination. The Western powers were able to prevent neither, which inevitably has had an effect upon the attitudes and the morale of the peoples of Eastern Europe. But it did not extinguish their feeling of affiliation with Western Europe, which became evident once the Communist regimes found it in their interest to open some doors to the outside world.

The Rigid Lines of the Cold War

Winston Churchill, in his famous speech at Fulton, Missouri, in 1946, had deplored the fate of the "capitals of the ancient states of central and eastern Europe . . . and the populations around them," cut off from the body of Europe by an iron curtain. Later in that same year, another Churchill speech at Zurich marked the start of the movement for European unity. So total had the separation from the East European states become, however, that all thoughts and plans "to recreate the European family, or as much of it as we can," were confined to the West.

The Communist seizure of power in Czechoslovakia in February 1948 had a double significance. First, it signaled the completion of Stalin's absorption of Eastern Europe in the Soviet Empire and was soon followed by the blockade of Berlin. Second, it convinced the nations of the West that they had to organize and arm in their own defense. There was no country left to serve as a "bridge" between East and West, a role which Edward Beneš and non-Communist Czech leaders had sought for their country. The Brussels Pact, or Western European Union, came into being in March, 1948, and the North Atlantic Treaty was signed in Washington within little more than a year after the coup in Prague. In 1950, the decision was taken to arm West Germany and to bring it into association with the Western alliance; meanwhile, the Soviets were incorporating East Germany into their own military bloc. Thus, at the height of the cold war in the early 1950s, two hostile systems confronted each other across the line which divided Germany and divided Europe. Each group of European nations was tied to an extra-European great power whose military strength dominated the coalition and held it together. Yet there were fundamental differences in the character of these two groups.

The Soviet security system in Eastern Europe had its foundation in omnipresent Soviet military power tied to political domination through satellite regimes. Moscow had bilateral treaties of alliance with each of these regimes. It controlled their armed forces. Although they had military alliances with each other, they did not and could not pursue independent policies, because ultimate control everywhere was in the hands of Stalin and his agents. When they did form a common treaty organization, the Warsaw Pact in 1955, there was no basic change. The system of bilateral treaties remained, and the

Warsaw Treaty Organization was no more than an instrument of Soviet policy. Of the East European states, only Yugoslavia escaped incorporation in the system by Tito's bold defiance of Stalin in 1948.

In the West, on the other hand, the nations of Europe began to come together for defense before they allied themselves formally with the United States. They entered into NATO of their own will. Seeing the need for greater unity for resolving their own pressing problems, they began a series of moves toward closer cooperation. The Council of Europe, established at Strasbourg, bore witness to the general desire. In the Organization for European Economic Cooperation, the countries receiving Marshall Plan aid acquired the habit of planning and working together. A series of moves by six states of continental Europe—France, West Germany, Italy, and the Benelux countries—went even to the point of some sacrifice of national sovereignty. The Schuman Plan brought into being a common organization for planning and control of their coal and steel industries. The proposed European Defense Community, a plan of French inspiration which eventually foundered on the rock of French opposition, was another illustration of the search for European rather than national solutions. The biggest step was the Treaty of Rome, signed in 1957, which established the European Economic Community (EEC), or Common Market, of the six continental nations. Its aim was, first, a customs union, and then a more comprehensive economic union. In this process, in which some aspects of sovereignty would gradually be yielded to supranational institutions, a growing political unity was implicit.

The edifice of Western European unity, in its early and critical stages, was the work of three extraordinary statesmen who were guiding the affairs of the three largest states of the area: Robert Schuman of France, Konrad Adenauer of the German Federal Republic, and Alcide de Gasperi of Italy. These three men were "Europeans" in thought and background. That is to say, they were Western Europeans; more narrowly, they were Western Europeans of a particular political persuasion, Christian Democracy. Thus, while they and their successors built a new Europe on the continent, it was a "little" Europe of the six nations, in which other West European states, including Great Britain, did not take part but organized themselves in the looser European Free Trade Area (EFTA). The more the community of the six moved toward integration, the more exclusive it tended to become. The nature of its association with other Western states, such as Britain, Austria, and Greece, was difficult enough to determine. Its leaders did not bother to give more than passing thought to relations with Eastern Europe.

It is remarkable how purely Western were the ideas of the prophets, and the approach of the practitioners, of European unity. The explanation lies partly in the fact that the East European countries were organized in a bloc which seemed to have nothing in common with the West and in fact was hostile to it. Thus, Western European unity had the purpose of defense against the East rather than reconciliation with it. Another consideration was political and economic ideology. There was no room for a state-trading Communist state in the EEC or in EFTA. Even the innocuous Council of Europe, which included neutral states such as Sweden, kept alive the idea of eventual membership for free East European nations, but issued no invitations to Communist governments to join. Yugoslavia, although not a member of the Soviet bloc, supported by the West in defending its independence against Soviet pressures, and cooperating with OEEC in a special status of associate, remained outside all the other "European" institutions.

During the early 1950s, with the lines of the cold war tightly drawn, the problem of Germany remained on the agenda of East-West negotiations, but no progress toward its solution was made. The status of Eastern Europe was not even discussed at the negotiating table. Despite talk of "liberation" coming from the United States, but not from Western Europe, Secretary Dulles was unable to have the subject placed on the agenda of the Geneva summit conference of 1955. At about this time, however, Khrushchev was consolidating his position in Russia, and the phrase "peaceful coexistence" began to be heard. As Soviet attention turned toward Asia and the Middle East, certain signs pointed toward possibilities of a relaxation of the total rigidity of the situation in Europe.

The Beginnings of Relaxation

The Soviet government agreed in 1955 to end the four-power occupation of Austria and to a slight drawing back of the line of Soviet military control in Europe, through conclusion of a state treaty and acceptance of Austrian neutrality. It made up its quarrel with Belgrade, on Tito's terms, thus confirming Yugoslavia's independence and its neutral position in the cold war. It surrendered the Soviet military base in Finland. These moves were accompanied by a propaganda barrage from Moscow on the need for peaceful coexistence. At the summit conference in Geneva, the Soviet Union and the three Western powers accepted something like a tacit agreement ruling out nuclear war as a practical instrument of policy for any power. At the same conference, Anthony Eden suggested in general terms a limitation on forces and armaments in Germany and a demilitarized zone of unspecified extent, as part of a settlement of the German question.

This was the first time that a proposal for "disengagement" was made at a high governmental level. It opened the door for many such proposals, official and unofficial, the most notable of which was Poland's Rapacki Plan, first put forward in 1957, for the "de-nuclearization" of West and East Germany, Poland, and Czechoslovakia. Moscow immediately endorsed it, and the Western powers, after mutual consultation, rejected it. Disengagement would have been most difficult to accept, in view of the complex military, political, and other factors involved. Almost any proposal contained, for one side or the other, risks greater than those involved in keeping the *status quo*. The most evenly balanced arrangement, moreover, would not reach the core of Europe's dangers and problems, for the confrontation of armed forces and the placement of nuclear weapons in certain areas were symptoms rather than causes of the cold war.

AUTONOMY AND DIVERSITY IN EASTERN EUROPE

However illusory, the talk of disengagement was indicative of a new atmosphere in Europe. Western nations began to show increased awareness that the interests of individual East European states might be different from those of the Soviet Union. The year 1956, with its dramatic events in Poland and Hungary, was indeed a decisive one for Eastern Europe. Although the Polish revolt against Soviet domination stopped half-way and the Hungarian revolt was crushed by Soviet arms, the Soviet empire was never the same again. It had been clearly demonstrated that the United States would not take the risk of using force in Eastern Europe, even when a nation was able temporarily to liberate itself. However, that did not mean that a rigid system of Soviet control could be re-established.

Poland had gained freedom to administer its own domestic affairs, within the limits of continuing rule by Wladislaw Gomulka and the Communist party, and even some slight independence in foreign policy. In Hungary Janos Kadar had been installed by Khrushchev and ruled as Khrushchev's man, but both of them had to take account of the mood of the Hungarian people and the need to obtain a minimum of cooperation from them to avoid economic disaster. Poland, in the period immediately following October 1956, opened up new contacts with the West: thousands of Poles were allowed to visit Western Europe, and economic aid was received from America. Hungary, after a couple of years of repression, began to ease pressures on the people and to permit travel to the West. Even the Romanian Communist leaders, who had stood loyally with Moscow in the Hungarian crisis, began to maneuver shortly thereafter to secure the withdrawal of Soviet troops from Romania, which took place in 1958, and to gain a more independent position.

Khrushchev was striving during the late 1950's to rebuild the Soviet bloc on a new basis, one which would substitute the common interests of the Communist regimes for the iron control exercised by Stalin. The Eastern European states would, of course, remain within the Soviet security system and would recognize the leading role of the Soviet Union. He gained a fair measure of success, but the very introduction of the idea of consent rather than dictation as the basis of Soviet-satellite relations was an invitation to the Eastern European states to negotiate or bargain on their own behalf rather than to submit automatically to a "line." When the Soviet-Chinese dispute broke into the open in 1960, the Eastern European states found more room to bargain and to maneuver. The "leading role" of Moscow could hardly carry its old political or moral authority when Peking was attacking it day after day in the press and over the radio.

ECONOMIC FACTORS

At this time, when "polycentrism" and diversity were making their appearance in the Communist world, Eastern Europe was experiencing a surge of economic growth and general prosperity. The advance took place just as the European Economic Community was getting established and moving, ahead of schedule, toward a customs union. How far the existence of the new Common Market was responsible for Western Europe's growing economic strength is a debatable question, but the two things were linked in the minds of people on both sides of Europe's line of partition.

The first Soviet response to the Common Market, judging from the Communist Party program of 1961 and from press comment, was to dismiss it as a last effort of the big monopolies of the fading capitalist system to save themselves by jointly exploiting a larger market, or as a new stage in the American exploitation of Western Europe.

However, as time went on, Soviet economists began to take a more objective look and to realize that Western Europe, if it continued to advance in unity and material growth, would be a formidable contender for influence and perhaps a dangerous opponent, especially if West Germany became the dominant force in it. Efforts were made to dissuade other European countries from joining and to warn third world countries against it as a new instrument of colonialism. What had happened could not but shake Soviet confidence in the superiority of socialism, especially at a time when the Soviet Union's rate of growth was slackening and some of the Eastern European states were encountering serious economic troubles. In Western Europe, especially in Italy, Communist parties and unions would not attack the Common Market using Soviet arguments because they found it a favorable development for their workers.

Sometime in 1962, Khrushchev decided on a new plan to integrate the economies of the Soviet bloc. It would be a reply to the integration of Western Europe, and at the same time could restore unity and discipline in the Communist camp—rather, that part of it still subject to Soviet influence, which did not include China or Albania —by economic means where political means had largely failed. The plan took shape at a meeting of the Council for Mutual Economic Assistance in June 1962, in which a set of principles of the international socialist division of labor was adopted. The basic idea, amplified by Khrushchev in a lengthy article written at the time, was to coordinate national plans in a master plan, have each country produce goods for which it was best suited, and thus maximize production in a "great socialist world market." Because of the size and wealth of the Soviet Union compared to the East European partners, there was little doubt where the powers of decision in drawing up and carrying out the master plan would lie.

The spearhead of resistance to economic integration of the Eastern bloc was Romania. Seeming an unlikely candidate for that role, having remained docile when Yugoslavia, Poland, and Hungary were asserting themselves against Moscow, Romania took a strong independent stand largely because its economy was more backward in development and more Stalinist in organization than most of the others. Its leaders feared that integration would confirm that status of inferiority and transfer powers of decision elsewhere. They were intent on proceeding with their own plans for rapid industrialization, regardless of what others might think about a proper international socialist division of labor. Romania, therefore, became the stalwart defender of the principle of national sovereignty at the council meetings of the CEMA in 1963. Since the rule of unanimity applied, that principle won the day. It was agreed that all arrangements for economic integration were to be voluntary, and that no member state was to be bound without its agreement.

The more industrialized Eastern European states, East Germany, Czechoslovakia, and Poland, apparently opposed Romania on the issues of greater integration, as they had an obvious desire to expand their own industries and their share of the market, but that any of them, with the possible exception of East Germany, really wanted to surrender control of decisions vitally affecting its own national economy to some supranational and probably Soviet-controlled body is open to serious question.

East-West Trade

One of the main reasons for rejecting integration with the East, the Romanians made clear, was the desire to trade with the West. They said they would sell their own goods and buy needed products wherever it was to their advantage to do so, anywhere in the world. Western equipment was desired by all the Eastern European states because of its quality, although they were not all equally able to obtain it, some being short of free currency or heavily dependent, economically, on the Soviet Union. Trade with Western Europe had continued, although at low levels, all through the period of the cold war, simply because Eastern Europe needed it. Much of it was replaced by trade within the bloc, especially with the Soviet Union. In the Khrushchev years, it increased steadily in volume although without much change in percentage of total trade, for exchanges with the U.S.S.R. and within Eastern Europe were also expanding. There were, however, considerable differences among the East European countries. Poland showed a decline in its trade with Western Europe between 1958 and 1965, while Romania showed a considerable rise, exports nearly doubling in those years. Czechoslovakia and Bulgaria, particularly, remain heavily dependent upon trade with Russia.

Eastern Europe's desire to trade across the iron curtain was matched by similar inclinations on the Western side. For some years, the nations of Western Europe had been chafing under the restrictions on trade with the East which had been applied in general agreement with the United States through a coordinating committee sitting in Paris. They saw less point in this kind of economic warfare as time went on; they found it more and more difficult to resist the pressure from their own business firms which wanted to deal with the East and they believed political influence might be gained as a by-product of trade. The export restrictions, accordingly, were gradually relaxed, with the reluctant agreement of the United States. Although the ban on arms and goods of a clearly military character was maintained, agreements for steel mills, electrical equipment, and machine tools went forward generally without hindrance and often on credit. It was an open competition, for there was no common Western policy either on the conditions of trade, including credit terms, or on whether and how trade might be used to further general policy ends. West Germany, because of its superior economic position, its historic trade ties with Eastern Europe, and its large volume of exchanges with Eastern Germany, led the way, despite political feuds and the absence of diplomatic relations with those states.

Three facts deserve special attention. First, Western Europe's trade with the states of Eastern Europe remains well above its trade with the Soviet Union and seems to be growing faster, an indication of closer mutual interest. Second, where nearly 20 per cent of Eastern Europe's trade is with Western Europe, the latter conducts less than 3 per cent of its total trade with Eastern Europe. If any conclusion can be drawn from that situation with respect to relative bargaining power through trade, the advantage would seem to be on the side of the West, especially since Western exports have been largely machinery and advanced equipment and Eastern exports largely foodstuffs and raw materials. Third, well over one-half of the trade of each Eastern European country, except Albania, has remained within the Soviet bloc, with the U.S.S.R. and other Eastern European states.

American trade with Eastern Europe has undergone no similar expansion and is dwarfed by the volume of Western Europe's trade. For example, American exports to Eastern Europe, excluding the U.S.S.R., in 1964 were $193 million, compared to Western Europe's $1,925 million; imports were $78 million, compared to Western Europe's $1,820 million. America's share in Eastern Europe's trade, moreover, has been swelled by extraordinary items, such as wheat shipments to Poland under Public Law 480, which are outside the normal channels of commercial relations.

Western Politics and Diplomacy

If trade has developed between the two halves of Europe more or less independently of political relationships, the two never were, and indeed could not be, kept in wholly separate compartments. Western policy toward Eastern Europe contained elements of common purpose and elements of diversity. As with trade, the economic recovery of Western Europe apparently brought with it almost inevitably the desire for greater independence from the United States in policy. Most striking in the case of France, the trend was evident in other nations as well. Diversity in the East was matched by diversity in the West. To understand the complexities of the new situation, it is necessary to see how the main issues in East-West relations were dealt with, on the Western side, since the end of World War II.

In the first decade after the end of the war, Western policy for all practical purposes was American policy. Western Europe was in a state of weakness, its attention riveted on recovery and on the challenge to the old colonial empires in Asia and Africa. France, a major power in Eastern Europe before the war, made no effort to restore its old influence. West Germany, emerging from allied occupation and tutelage under the political leadership of Adenauer, hoped for German reunification, but made acceptance as an equal partner in the Western community the primary aim of its diplomacy. Britain saw its interests as a world power best served by close cooperation with the United States, as both were threatened by the outward thrust of Soviet power.

EASTERN EUROPE AND THE GERMAN QUESTION

The major issues of contention with the Soviet Union in Europe were the situation in Eastern Europe and the future status of Germany. The peace treaties with Hungary, Romania and Bulgaria, negotiated by the Soviet Union and the three major Western powers and signed in 1947, did not remove Western objections to Soviet domination of those countries through satellite governments. The United States and Great Britain registered disapproval of the measures by which actual and potential opposition to Soviet-Communist rule was destroyed in all the countries of Eastern Europe, whether they had been wartime allies or former enemy states. France joined them in condemning the Communist seizure of Czechoslovakia in

1948. All three supported Yugoslavia in its defiance of Moscow in the years after 1948. In 1953, at Bermuda, the three Western governments again recorded their conviction that Soviet domination of the nations of Eastern Europe was neither just nor permanent. But this was a matter of aspiration and not of policy. In Eastern Europe, the Western nations had no bargaining power, for Russia was in authority. In Germany, they had such power, in the form of military forces stationed in the larger and more important part of that country and the cooperation of the West German government. It was assumed that little, if anything, could be done about Eastern Europe until a settlement was first reached on Germany. Thus, the main subject for negotiation with the Soviet Union over these years was always the same: Germany and a German peace treaty, including the question of Berlin, the focal point of periodic crises.

The four major powers, the United States, Britain, France and the Soviet Union, began negotiating on Germany at Moscow in the spring of 1947. They continued at London in the same year, Paris in 1949, Berlin in 1954, Geneva twice in 1955, and Geneva again in 1959. They discussed, among other things, unification of Germany, creation of a central German government, frontiers, and terms of a peace treaty. They agreed on nothing. The first step, a formula to bring West and East Germany together so that there could be a single German government to sign the peace treaty, could not be taken for the simple reason that the Soviet Union was not willing to release East Germany, or to allow the Germans to choose an all-German government by a free election, which would have produced the same result. So there was no peace settlement. The German Federal Republic became a sovereign state and full-fledged partner of the Western nations in NATO and in the various European organizations, notably the Common Market. Eastern Germany, christened the "German Democratic Republic" but unrecognized by any but Communist states, became a full-fledged member of the Soviet bloc while remaining the main base of Soviet military power in Central Europe.

With the persisting division of Germany, which meant also the continuance of the dangerous situation of West Berlin as a free island in a Communist sea, the issue of German reunification remained a possibly explosive one, a barrier to understanding between Western and Eastern Europe. Another barrier has been the unsettled question of Germany's eastern frontiers. At the Potsdam Conference in 1945, the line dividing the Soviet zone of occupation in Germany from the territories handed over to Polish administration was set along the course of the Oder and Western Neisse rivers. This drastic decision made by Stalin was accepted by the Western powers, "subject to confirmation at the peace settlement." They could do nothing to change it if they had wanted to. From the start, the Soviet and Polish governments, and later the East German regime, regarded the Potsdam decision as having established the final frontier. The United States and Great Britain, and later the Bonn government, took the position that the Oder-Neisse line was only provisional until confirmed, or changed, by a general peace treaty with Germany. In the absence of a treaty and with Germany divided, it is scarcely an explosive frontier, since it runs between Poland and East Germany, two fraternal Communist states, but Bonn's refusal to accept it as the final Polish-German frontier continues to envenom relations between Poland and the Federal Republic, Great Britain and the United States.

The Geneva conference of 1959 was the last attempt to reach a negotiated solution of the German question. Khrushchev continued to exert pressure on Berlin, where tension rose to the point of a real war scare in 1961. Since the Cuban missile crisis of 1962, however, both sides have chosen to live with the *status quo* rather than risk war to change it. The Soviet Union signed a new treaty with the East German regime in June 1964, giving it military guarantees, and has sought in every possible way to win international acceptance for that regime. Meanwhile, the Western nations continue to refuse it recognition and to maintain the right of the people in both parts of Germany to reunification on the basis of free elections.

Acknowledgment that no general negotiated settlement on Germany was possible did not mean that quiet and stability would descend upon Central and Eastern Europe. As the situation there was not static but dynamic, the main question was how the various forces at work would affect, or would be affected by, the policies of the principal nations concerned. The Soviet tactic of "peaceful coexistence," the apparent fading of any Soviet military threat to Western Europe, and the general loosening of the Eastern bloc all combined to encourage Western European nations to seek policies of their own toward the East instead of a united front under American leadership. In the 1960s, one could hardly speak of a common Western policy on Germany and Western Europe, except at the moment of crisis when Khrushchev threatened war over Berlin. Other than the general commitment under the North Atlantic Treaty for common defense, there were different national policies pursued by individual Western governments. It is therefore necessary, in considering the future of East-West relations in Europe, to take into account the policies which have been developing in London, Paris, and Bonn.

GREAT BRITAIN

Britain's policy toward Russia, Eastern Europe, and the German question has reflected its changing, and often ambiguous, position as a world power: partnership with, and dependence on, the United States, in maintaining certain global positions; the desire to play a leading role in Europe, but without becoming "European" at the cost of severing special ties with the Commonwealth and the United States; official support of Germany's right to unity in freedom, tempered by less than cordial relations with the Bonn government and widespread anti-German feelings among the British people; opposition to Soviet imperialism and expansion, coupled with a fascination for the role of mediator and peacemaker when Soviet moves and demands threaten the peace.

In the first years after World War II, the Labour government, with Ernest Bevin as Foreign Secretary, stood solidly with the United States in protesting the imposition of Soviet control in Eastern Europe, strengthening the Western position in Germany, and defending the right of the Germans to unity in freedom. The Conservative government, which came to power in 1951, continued the same policies, though an almost desperate public and official belief in negotiation acquired acceptance as the answer to East-West tension and controversy, even when there was no apparent basis for agreement. Thus, Anthony Eden, with an election in the offing, obtained his summit conference in 1955, which produced little more than the "spirit of Geneva." Similarly, Harold Macmillan, after a pilgrimage to Moscow, obtained his conference on Berlin and Germany in 1959, the only notable outcome of which was Khrushchev's visit to the United States.

The idea of disengagement, meanwhile, had captivated the Labour party, whose leader, Hugh Gaitskell, put out a number of proposals along the lines of a modified Rapacki Plan, although the British government never committed itself to a specific plan of disengagement. During the prolonged Berlin crisis brought on by Khrushchev's reopening of the question with an "ultimatum" in 1958, the British toyed with a number of compromise proposals which included *de facto* recognition of the East German regime. At that time, the

United States was also giving attention to possible compromise settlements. Here again, however, the British government did not separate itself from its Western partners.

It is not easy to evaluate British policy and diplomacy over the years. The most favorable interpretation is that, while maintaining a general solidarity with other Western nations on the basic principles at issue with the Soviet Union, it has shown a flexibility which, in contrast to the stiff position of the United States and West Germany, has helped to surmount dangerous crises in Europe without war and without vital concessions. The least favorable interpretation is that, without taking a really independent line, British policy has operated within the Western alliance as an element of weakness and even appeasement, encouraging Soviet demands and intransigence when greater firmness in the West might have had the opposite effect. There can be, of course, many other interpretations, but one conclusion seems clear: at no time since the war has British policy had a decisive or even a major influence with regard to the problem of Germany and the future of Eastern Europe, whether the government has been led by Attlee or Churchill, by Eden, Macmillan, Douglas-Home, or Wilson. In the general state of movement and change now evident in Europe, Britain may have a more important and more independent role to play than in the past. To date, the great example of independence of policy has been not Britain, but France.

FRANCE

Under the Fourth Republic, France had no policy in Eastern Europe other than general support of Western positions in the cold war. As to Germany, after early attempts to gain special positions in the Ruhr and Saar, the French came to the conclusion that reconciliation with the Bonn Republic offered the best hope for future security. They supported the general Western positions on Germany in the various negotiations with the Soviet Union. When General de Gaulle came to power in 1958, he made no change. In fact, he chose to build his European policy on close cooperation with Germany; France became the firmest supporter of Bonn and of German interests in the recurrent crises over Berlin. In January 1963, this policy of reconciliation and rapprochement culminated in the French-German treaty of friendship, which provided for something like a common policy in foreign affairs, defense, and economic and cultural matters, although without great expectation that it was a practical, or even desirable, proposition in existing circumstances; France has continued to support the principle of German reunification. General de Gaulle, in building a new role for his own country, has refused to tie his policies to the interests of any other country. At the same time that he was building the new relationship with Bonn, he was forming his own conceptions about policy toward the Soviet Union and Eastern Europe.

General de Gaulle, consistently since the Second World War, has championed the idea of the rebirth of Europe in its great role in history, lost at the Yalta Conference where, unrepresented and temporarily weak, it could not prevent the division of the continent by Russia and America. In the early years after returning to power, he left no doubt that he did not accept the East European satellite governments as truly representative of their peoples. Thus, Soviet domination would have to end before Europe could recover its proper place in the world. De Gaulle's world is one of nations, and he has rejected Soviet hegemony over the nations of Eastern Europe just as he rejected what he considers American hegemony in Western Europe. But his concept of the Europe of the future, extending "from the Atlantic to the Urals," seemed to accept the U.S.S.R., or European Russia at any rate, as one of the European family of nations, at the same time that it questioned Great Britain's European credentials and rejected the influence of the United States. An integral part of the concept was that Moscow must cease to threaten, America must cease to control Western Europe's strategy and policies through NATO, and the cold war must be brought to an end. Russia, given adequate assurance of its own security and evolving toward greater freedom, would have no further reason to occupy part of Germany or to dominate Eastern European nations. It could, then, cooperate with France in building the new *Europe des patries.*

What all this has to do with the realities of international politics, or the interests of the French people, is a legitimate question. A Europe containing the Soviet Union and a united Germany would hardly look for leadership to Paris. This consideration illuminates de Gaulle's remark that "Europe's daughter, America" would not be totally out of the picture, but would still be a counterweight. Thus, he has repudiated NATO but not the North Atlantic Treaty itself.

However many the questions that may be raised, it would be a mistake to dismiss Gaullist pronouncements on the future, in view of the record the General has compiled in pursuing his ideas by single-minded diplomacy and action. He has succeeded in gravely weakening NATO, in barring British entry into the Common Market, and in checking the movement toward greater Western European unity. What he has been able to accomplish in Eastern Europe is less apparent but may be of considerable importance in its effects on the calculations and the policies of other powers.

Encouraged by signs of increased independence on the part of the East European nations since 1958, General de Gaulle has decided to treat them as fully sovereign states and to court the favor of their governments. He has stated his support of the Oder-Neisse line as the permanent frontier between Germany and Poland. He has welcomed a series of East European prime ministers and foreign ministers to Paris, where the idea of Europe has regularly been invoked. Couve de Murville, his Minister of Foreign Affairs, has visited the East European capitals, signing agreements on trade, economic cooperation, and cultural exchange. The French "presence" has now returned to Eastern Europe, not in its prewar form but as a means of turning détente into entente, as the French themselves have put it.

All this French activity in Eastern Europe need not be regarded as incompatible with the interests of other Western nations. It may contribute to them by swelling the currents of contact with the West, for France in the past has often been the very center and spirit of Western civilization to Poles, Hungarians, Romanians, and others in Eastern Europe. The greater the flow of goods, persons, and ideas, the greater the total influence of the West, even though the motivation of some of the East European governments may be primarily to serve Soviet strategy. What is more critical, from the general standpoint of Western interests, is the relationship between Gaullist France and the Soviet Union.

President de Gaulle visited the Soviet Union in June, 1966, and Prime Minister Kosygin returned the visit later in the same year. The visits produced no alliances or treaties, but only speeches and communiqués in which both sides paid tribute to peace, coexistence, and European security. However, de Gaulle's opening to the East had additional significance. It was a personal and national venture, in no way coordinated with other Western governments. Though avoiding endorsement of the Soviet plan for an all-European security conference, he agreed with his hosts at Moscow "that the problem of Europe should first of all be discussed within the limits of Europe." The statement on the importance of "regular contacts that would enable leading Soviet and French statesmen to discuss problems of mutual interest with a view to coordinating their positions," which appeared in the joint communiqué issued at the end of Kosygin's visit, seemed to say that the President recognized no such thing as a general Western or West European policy. It was a demonstration of his view that France could be the spokesman for Western Europe, and that with the current leader in the Kremlin he could somehow settle the fate of Europe, as Napoleon and Czar Alexander I tried to do at Tilsit in 1807.

The exclusion of America and perhaps even of Britain from influence in Europe was hardly an idea to be welcomed by the many other European nations, including those of Eastern Europe. Although de Gaulle did not accept Soviet views on the German question, the whole atmosphere of revival of the Franco-Russian alliance of former years was bound to raise questions among the Germans as to what had happened to their 1963 treaty of friendship and their permanent reconciliation with France. A dash of realism, perhaps, was the best antidote. It was true that the opportunities which French policy offered to the Soviets further to exploit the disunity of the West held some immediate dangers. But France was not prepared to be a pawn in a purely Soviet strategy.

There was no evidence, moreover, that de Gaulle could force his own policy on other Western European nations, or that he had the authority and power to represent Western Europe (or perhaps even the France of five years hence), or that the Soviet leaders accepted him in that role. They certainly did not share his dream of the future Europe, and they gave no indication that they had abandoned the long-standing Soviet conviction that the key to Europe lies not in France, but in Germany.

THE FEDERAL REPUBLIC OF GERMANY

The German Federal Republic's policy on the future of Eastern Europe differs from that of other Western nations for the obvious reason that Germany's own future is directly involved. Germany is an object as well as a subject in this particular international problem, for a part of the German nation, the Soviet-occupied zone, is functioning as a Communist state within the Soviet bloc. Reunification of Germany through self-determination is a prime political objective of the Federal Republic, and in the eyes of the other Western powers it has been the essential first step for a settlement of the German question. But a first step which would liquidate East Germany has met unswerving opposition from the Soviet Union, because it would mean loss of an important strategic position, of what is economically the strongest state in the Soviet bloc after the Soviet Union itself, and possibly, of what remains of Soviet political power and prestige in the whole of Eastern Europe. It is not surprising that the only German unity Moscow is prepared to see is a united Communist Germany.

In the face of this fixed Soviet position, East-West negotiations on Germany were bound to fail. The West could and did resist Soviet and East German pressure on West Berlin, but it could not open up for real negotiation the wider question of ending the division of Germany, which was the only context in which the Berlin problem could be solved. The division of Germany, in turn, was but one part, albeit the most explosive one, of the division of Europe, which gave no sign of yielding to negotiation.

In the period of Adenauer's leadership, which lasted until 1963, West Germany gave priority to becoming an equal member of the Western community and building a close relationship with the United States. Reunification was a declared goal, but Adenauer had no "eastern policy" as a means of attaining it; rather, he counted on the growing strength of the West eventually to force the Soviet Union to give up East Germany. His government saw nothing to be gained toward reunification by negotiation with the Soviets or by opening up channels to the Communist states of Eastern Europe. Bonn clung to the so-called Hallstein doctrine, under which it had no diplomatic relations with any state recognizing the East German regime, except the Soviet Union, as one of the major victorious Allied powers. All the Soviet satellites had recognized that regime from the start, and when Yugoslavia took the same step in 1957, Bonn promptly broke off relations with Belgrade. There were moments in the 1950s when opportunities appeared for increased trade and other contacts between the Federal Republic and individual East European states, as in the period following the events of October 1956 in Poland. But neither Adenauer nor Gomulka thought it worthwhile to pursue the matter very far.

The appearance of Gerhard Schröder as Foreign Minister under Chancellor Erhard in 1963 gave a voice on the cabinet level to those in the diplomatic service, the business community, and elsewhere who had been urging an opening to the east. The Federal Republic then set about fostering trade with the states of Eastern Europe. It established trade missions in Warsaw, Budapest, Bucharest, and

Sofia which became channels of intergovernmental communication short of the diplomatic level. The way was thus paved for Erhard's successor, early in 1967, to exchange embassies with Romania, Bonn finally showing sufficient flexibility to circumvent the Hallstein doctrine and Bucharest demonstrating its independence and rejecting the objections of Moscow and of Ulbricht's regime in East Germany.

In Hungary, Romania, and Bulgaria, the Federal Republic did not encounter the same wall of hostility it met in dealing with Poland and Czechoslovakia, where anti-German feeling was rooted in centuries of rivalry and conflict, intensified manyfold by the German occupation during World War II. Poland and Germany also had between them the burning question of the Oder-Neisse line, and Czechoslovakia had the grievance of German reluctance formally to repudiate once and for all the Munich agreement of 1938. Although Schröder left the foreign ministry when the "big coalition" government of Christian Democrats and Social Democrats took office in November 1966, the "eastern policy" was even more strongly emphasized by the new Chancellor, Kurt Georg Kiesinger, and the new Foreign Minister, Willy Brandt. Kiesinger wasted no time in giving the Czechs the assurance that the Bonn government regarded the Munich agreement as no longer valid, though remaining silent on the question whether it ever had been. As for Poland, he spoke of reconciliation and "a freely agreed settlement with an all-German government" as a basis for good-neighborly relations, but made no move on the Oder-Neisse line. In general terms, Kiesinger added Germany to the list of nations appointing themselves to the role of "bridge" between Western and Eastern Europe. The establishment of diplomatic relations with Romania marked a notable advance, but no other East European state immediately followed Bucharest's lead, and Poland declared it would be unthinkable unless Bonn accepted both the Oder-Neisse line and the sovereignty of the East German state.

Whether a West German declaration accepting the Oder-Neisse line as the frontier of a future united Germany would make any great difference in the present state of affairs is an open question. There is no real expectation in West Germany, except perhaps among refugee elements, that the German nation will recover any of the territories east of the Oder and the Neisse. However, no politician has felt able to take such a position in public, and the legal claim to the 1937 frontiers is regarded as a bargaining point for the future, so Bonn has gone no farther than to pledge it will not use force to try to change existing *de facto* boundaries. The big coalition, not having to face any strong opposition, might be in a position to recognize the frontier. There is some doubt, however, that the Gomulka regime in Warsaw or the Soviet government would like to see Bonn accept the Oder-Neisse line, for it is the main issue they have in convincing the Polish people that they have no alternative but to look to their present regime and to Moscow for protection against a revanchist Germany bent on robbing Poland of its new territories.

Remaining unsettled, and incessantly agitated, the frontier question has stood as an insuperable barrier to normal or friendly relations between the Federal Republic and Poland. And the relationship of these two countries is central to the success of any West German policy aimed at reunification and at rapprochement with Eastern Europe. It is hard to see how an eastern policy aimed at better relations with East European states can resolve this particular issue, unless there is some basic change in the positions of the Polish and Soviet governments. Another kind of eastern policy is a "Rapallo policy" aimed at an understanding with the Soviet Union, the only power able to give Germany the prize of reunification, perhaps at Poland's expense. In either case the key is in Russian hands.

Conclusions

The variety of aims and policies pursued by the different Western nations indicates how difficult it would be for the West to deal in a single or coordinated way with the East European states and the Soviet Union. There is no agreed Atlantic approach, although the United States and some allies in NATO have begun to give lip service to the general idea. The NATO Council in December 1966 endorsed the idea of détente but noted that varying approaches to the East could be adopted, "whether between individual countries or in a wider international framework." Admittedly, a solid NATO approach to negotiations with the Warsaw Pact countries, which the Secretary-General of NATO said was not envisaged, tends to evoke a common Soviet and East European response from the other side. A greater flexibility and independence for Western Europe, within the broad confines of the Atlantic alliance, might be more likely to encourage the Eastern European states to separate themselves to some degree from Moscow.

WHAT KIND OF NEW EUROPE?

As we have seen, however, there is no agreed Western European approach, although it is not beyond the bounds of possibility that some greater degree of coordination in political strategy might be attained. General de Gaulle, in conducting his policy of independence, has attacked the institutional solidarity not only of NATO but of the EEC and other European institutions. By checking progress toward political unity in Western Europe, he has preserved a looser structure with which East European states eventually might find some links, but at the same time made it less likely that Western Europe can act together in meeting such contingencies. Great Britain, torn by the question of "joining Europe" or not, has been in no position to give a strong lead to any of its partners in policy toward Eastern Europe. Germany inevitably sees eastern policy primarily as a means of moving toward reunification. And the United States, with global responsibilities and its intense concentration on Vietnam, has not provided strong leadership. Its policy of "bridge-building" leaves open the choice among fundamentally different strategies: rebuilding the solidarity of the West, while trying to induce individual East European states to move toward a status of neutrality or toward association with the West; cooperating with Moscow to find a more stable global and European balance between the two powers, in which both Western and Eastern Europe will find their place; or building a new Europe (in the West alone or including East European states) capable of standing on its own feet, independent of both peripheral powers.

Thus, uncertainty in the policy of most governments concerned has reflected the fluidity of the situation. Everybody was talking about "Europe," but no country seemed to be going there. A Europe including the Soviet Union and bound to be dominated by it would not be acceptable to the West, while a powerful Europe extending to the Soviet borders would not be acceptable to Moscow. If there were to be a big Europe, succeeding the little Europe built in the West and the former group of Soviet satellites in the East, it obviously would not and could not take the shape of either. Even in the most optimistic view, how closely could the two parts of the continent, excluding Russia, be drawn together? Aside from historical, ideological, and institutional differences, the mere loosening of ties with the United States on the one side and with the Soviet Union on the other would not necessarily lead to relationships of

close association. The cult of national sovereignty which weakened
the alliance system was no constructive or integrating force. The
prospect of a big Europe, indeed, rested largely on the restoration
of something like the prewar system of national states. What kind
of security arrangements would contain the nationalist pressures and
rivalries inherent in such a system?

Projects for a European security treaty or nonaggression pact, on
Soviet initiative, had been on the agenda of the four-power conferences of the 1950's and were brought up from time to time since
then, but no serious discussion on the subject could be held because
of the total incompatibility of views on Germany. The Soviets saw in
their various proposals a means of sealing their grip on East Germany,
obtaining its recognition, destroying NATO (for which they were
willing to give up the Warsaw Pact), neutralizing Germany while
keeping it divided, and introducing a collective guarantee which
could not be effective without Soviet consent. The Western powers,
except perhaps France, were not ready to accept the change in the
strategic balance which a withdrawal of American forces back across
the Atlantic would bring, even if Soviet forces withdrew from Eastern Europe. They saw no point in a treaty which did no more than
repeat the principles and obligations of the UN Charter, and real
danger in one in which faith in Soviet cooperation replaced the
hard guarantees of the North Atlantic Treaty.

In 1966, the proposal was heard again, for the Soviet Union, with
the later endorsement of its Warsaw Pact partners, proposed an all-
Europe security conference to conclude such a treaty. This struck a
somewhat responsive chord, because, in addition to the Soviets, General de Gaulle and others had begun to talk about Europeans'
settling Europe's destiny. The theme has also been taken up by some
of the smaller states on both sides and in the middle. At the UN
General Assembly session of 1965, Romania introduced a resolution
encouraging contacts among smaller European states in the cause of
good neighborly relations and peace. The resolution was eventually
sponsored by nine states: Austria, Sweden, Finland and Yugoslavia in
the middle position, in addition to Denmark and Belgium on the
western side and Hungary, Romania and Bulgaria on the eastern. It
was passed unanimously by the General Assembly. The Yugoslavs,
grasping at the chance to assert leadership in the cause of coexistence
and easing of cold war tensions, set out to organize a meeting of
members of the parliaments of the nine states with the idea of push-
ing the proposal further. But it would be a long time before such a

group, even if well organized, could exert a decisive influence on the European scene. The effect of its organization might be only to weaken the solidarity of Western Europe.

These initiatives, whether from small nations or large, have tended to encourage closer relations between the two parts of Europe. Call it coexistence or peaceful engagement or détente, the theme is a recognition of the fact that merely maintaining military strength and talking endlessly about the German problem brought Europe no closer to security or to a political settlement. While the Western nations obviously must be on guard against allowing the Soviets to gain by a soft policy what they could not win by threats, they owe it to themselves to test whether the new emphasis on drawing Europe together, evident among nations on both sides, could open the way to changed relationships, to a real modification of security needs, and perhaps, as a final step, to the peaceful reunification of Germany. The difficulty has been that the considerations of power which thus far have blocked German unity and required the continued existence of NATO have undergone no fundamental transformation.

PROSPECTS

So long as the Soviet Union regards control of East Germany essential to its security and is not brought by radical internal or international changes to alter that view, it will no doubt resist changes in Eastern Europe which tend to undermine that control. Moreover, so long as the Soviet policy of peaceful coexistence is a strategy in competition for power by means short of war, the basic security of the Western world and the possibility of negotiating on an equal basis will continue to lie in an irreducible minimum of Western solidarity and in the presence of American power in Europe. The Soviet Union, so far as the evidence shows, still sees a "settlement" only in terms which are at least as favorable to it as the *status quo,* while the major Western allies cannot regard a divided Germany and the continued military confrontation as any stable settlement at all. Given that framework, the states of Western and Eastern Europe can pursue closer relations and greater unity only within certain definite limits.

In the absence of some basic shift in Soviet policy, can Eastern European states by themselves move toward peaceful engagement with the West? Here the increasing movement of goods and of persons across the line of partition is of great importance. It may be the only way that a new political climate, in which the partition itself could fade and disappear, may eventually be brought into being. The Soviet Union, which has already seen its dominant position weakened, might swallow more of the same medicine if it came in small doses. The Communist states of the Balkans, which are not so central to Soviet security, could possibly make a transition to a neutral position and to normal relations with the West; states like Austria and Yugoslavia, because of their middle position and their ties with both sides, might have a significant role to play. For Poland and Czechoslovakia, where the Soviet Union sees its own security directly at stake, such a change would be much more difficult.

Much depends on developments within the East European states themselves. There is still a gap between the regimes and the peoples. For the former, the course of rapprochement with Western Europe, though they have deliberately undertaken to expand contacts, is not without its dangers. When in need, they may look to Moscow for ultimate support. A real coming together of the two parts of Europe, therefore, should have behind it on the eastern side more than a desire for greater freedom of action on the part of the governments and for more trade and cultural exchanges. It may have to await a further closing of the gap between basically insecure regimes and the peoples whom they govern.

Robert F. Byrnes

7

American Opportunities and Dilemmas

The Soviet Union acquired military authority over Eastern Europe, except Yugoslavia, during the closing days of the Second World War, when its armies advanced through the area as they destroyed Nazi influence and strength. Between 1945 and 1953, Stalin established firm Soviet control through skillful policies which weakened and then obliterated rival political organizations and institutions; acquired control over and manipulated the armies and police systems; placed the economies under the grip of Communists loyal to the Soviet Union; redirected the economies and trade to the advantage of the Soviet Union; transformed the cultural life by suppressing the churches, by placing the educational systems under Communist authority, and by making socialist realism the effective cultural policy; and began the transformation of each country into a society modeled upon that of the Soviet Union. By the time of Stalin's death on March 5, 1953, the Soviet Union had made such progress in fastening its authority over Eastern Europe and in reshaping the area that many western observers abandoned hope that it would one day again be free.

However, the death of Stalin, the decisions made by his successors, and the gradual unbinding of Soviet control have so transformed the situation in Eastern Europe that within fifteen years the weakening of Soviet control and the decline of Soviet influence had become visible. The rulers of the Soviet Union will seek vigorously to maintain the political monopoly now established by Communist parties loyal to the Soviet Union and will seek to retain control over the foreign policies of those states still associated with the Russians. The Soviet Union will also seek to maintain and strengthen the economic, political, and cultural ties to the Soviet Union, but the Soviet leaders must recognize that these ties are not so vigorous as they were and that Soviet influence in these areas is likely to continue to wither.

The remarkable decline of the Soviet presence in Eastern Europe reflects a number of factors which Americans must review carefully when reaching decisions concerning future policy. Perhaps the most important reason for the change is that Eastern Europe can no longer be isolated as it was. The same factors which have made the world smaller for us and which have opened the United States to external influences also affect Eastern Europe, which every day becomes again more a part of Europe and the world.

The vigorous revival of nationalism throughout Eastern Europe has also played a prominent role in the recent changes. The most outstanding example, of course, is Yugoslavia, which now has a national Communist system. Albania is just as vigorous in its independence from the Soviet Union as Yugoslavia, although its political and economic system and external relationships differ markedly. Romania is seeking to become economically independent of the Soviet Union, and the governments of the other Eastern European states are moving in the same direction, although slowly and fitfully.

The very successes of the Communists in transforming Eastern Europe have also helped produce some of the significant changes. Thus, the expansion of industry and of the bureaucracy has created a large new class of administrators, managers, engineers, and intellectuals whose interests are quite different from those of the group which helped install Soviet power in the late 1940's or from those who served in the 1950's. In addition, the new young generation, aware of the difference between doctrine and reality and discontented with economic and cultural arrangements, has helped revise the established system. The attempted revolt in Hungary in the fall of 1956, led by the darlings of the Soviet system, the workers, the students, and the intellectuals, reflected those burgeoning forces, which are now attaining more modest goals in a more discrete fashion.

Soviet control has been weakened also by the reactions caused by the shift in Soviet policies after Stalin. Briefly, Stalin's successors chose to be more loved than feared, and the relaxation which they established and the greater freedom they gave to the national Communist regimes have led to economic and social developments of far-reaching significance. For example, the gradually increased emphasis on consumer goods, improved living standards, legality, and expanded relations with foreign countries have all fed the appetites of East Europeans and created more quiet pressures within their ruling groups as well as against their governments and the Soviet Union. Furthermore, the economic development of these countries has created great strains within the countries and between them and the Soviet Union. Some, particularly Romania and the more advanced industrial countries, seek industrial equipment of high quality from the West and also seek markets there for their goods, which they often prefer or need to sell for hard currencies.

The economic development of Eastern Europe and the appearance of new economic problems has also deposed or tilted the ideology of Marxism-Leninism, which to many communist leaders in Eastern Europe seems totally irrelevant for the last third of the twentieth century. This subtle challenge to the official ideology has been vastly strengthened by Soviet pronunciations of new doctrines. The idea of peaceful coexistence, the dogma that there are now several roads to socialism and that the Soviet Union no longer is the sole model, and the doctrine that socialism can be obtained by peaceful means have all shaken the confidence of Communists in their faith and have weakened the hold of ideology throughout the Communist system.

The withering away of the old faith has been strengthened and is reflected in developments within the international Communist movement, particularly the open dispute between the Soviet Union and the Chinese People's Republic. This conflict between the two greatest Communist states has weakened all of the binding ties, created opportunities for skillful political maneuvering, and helped produce doctrines known as revisionism and polycentrism. In short, the destruction of the myth of international Communist unity and the open frictions within the movement have had a very powerful influence within Eastern Europe and upon the relations between the states of the area and the Soviet Union.

Soviet domination over Eastern Europe has also been weakened by Western Europe's remarkable recovery in economic, political, military, and intellectual vitality. Stalin thought that a socialist Eastern Europe would draw Western Germany and then all of Western Europe into its system by the sheer magnetism which the "people's democracies" were to develop. However, the magnetism is flow-ing in exactly the reverse direction, because the dynamism of Western Europe has attracted the interest and fascination of the peoples and governments of Eastern Europe. The growing gap between Western Europe and Eastern Europe at a time when increased information is available has made East Europeans more than ever aware of their past membership in the European world and anxious to take advantage of the opportunities which Western Europe offers.

Finally, of course, developments within Eastern Europe have been immensely affected by the continued growth of every aspect of American power and by both the skill and resolution with which the United States has used its strength to defend and assist its allies and to contain the massive outthrust of Soviet power. The American shield or umbrella over Western Europe has mightily affected Eastern Europe, but containment was adopted late, has often been criticized or challenged, and by itself will clearly be inadequate in the years ahead.

Containment—Liberation—Disengagement

CONTAINMENT

American policy toward Eastern Europe has changed as changes have occurred within that complex area. During the last two years of the Second World War and until 1947, the policy of the United States might accurately be described as appeasement, because President Roosevelt and President Truman, and most Americans, were eager to demonstrate to the Soviet leaders that the United States had no ambitions which would threaten the vital interests of the Soviet Union and that we were immensely eager to live on peaceful terms with the Russians. The fastening of Soviet rule on Eastern Europe led to a change in 1947 defined as containment, which was enunciated first by George Kennan. This policy reflected the conviction that the continued expansion of Soviet power had to be resisted "with unalterable counter-force at every point where they [the Russians] show signs of encroaching upon the interests of a peaceful and stable world." It rested on the assumption that successful containment of Communist expansion would "increase enormously the strains under which Soviet policy must operate, to force upon the Kremlin a far greater degree of moderation and circumspection than it has had to observe in recent years, and in this way to promote tendencies which must eventually find their outlet in either the breakup or the gradual mellowing of Soviet power."

Containment was based upon the increase of American and allied military strength, the economic and political recovery of Western Europe, progress toward some form of unifying economic and political organization of the West European states, and above all, the demonstration by the United States and its allies of their determination to resist Communist expansion by force, when necessary, as in Greece, Korea, and South Viet Nam. The principal organization reflecting this search for strength in unity was the North Atlantic Treaty Organization, or NATO, which has become the armed umbrella under which Western Europe has been freed from Soviet pressure and enabled to grow in peace.

The West's growing strength and unity have enabled it to make effective use of diplomacy and of its other resources. The most striking opportunity, which was at the same time a dilemma for the American people, was offered by Yugoslavia, which was ousted from the Cominform in June, 1948, and toward which the United States and its allies have acted with remarkably good sense and high skills. In other words, Western economic and military assistance has enabled Tito, the "successful heretic," to maintain the unity and coherence of Yugoslavia against the various pressures which the Soviet Union has sought to direct against him and his Communist state. Western relations with Tito have not been uniformly friendly, and many Americans have wondered about the wisdom of aiding a Communist; but Western diplomacy has been exercised with such restraint that Yugoslavia has been able to survive as an independent state, serving therefore as an example to other Communist states of what vigorous national leadership can achieve and of the probable American and Western policies toward other states which seek increased national independence.

LIBERATION

In spite of the remarkable achievements of containment, a great deal of dissatisfaction existed in the United States by 1952 because of its limitations and various failures. For example, many noted that the Soviet Union had established itself on what Lenin used to call the commanding heights in Eastern Europe and that prospects for the area were even more bleak than they had been in 1947. They realized that the Soviet Union had acquired control over the police and armed forces and was engaged in reshaping the cultural values of the conquered peoples, developing heavy industrial bases in each country, promoting agricultural collectivization, exploiting the area efficiently, and using Eastern Europe as an instrument of pressure against Western Europe and Yugoslavia. Moreover, these apparent achievements and the seizure of power by the Chinese Communists led to the belief among Communists and among many opposed to communism that communism could be controlled only if it were forcefully pushed back. Finally, of course, Soviet control of Eastern Europe, particularly of Eastern Germany, gave the Soviet Union a strong and apparently firm advanced base in central Europe, divided the very heart of Europe, and provided Russia a veto on any proposals for the reunification of Germany and therefore of the unification of Europe itself.

Some Americans therefore turned briefly against containment. Thus the policy of the American government from early 1953 through the summer of 1954 was labeled *liberation,* and President Eisenhower and his colleagues often spoke of liberating Eastern Europe and of rolling back Communist power with a "positive foreign policy," which was generally believed to mean increased application of external pressure on the Soviet system until its collapse produced the emancipation of the peoples under Soviet domination. The policy of liberation frightened our friends and allies, enabled Communists throughout the world to portray the United States as an aggressive militaristic power, and had no apparent effect upon the power or policy of the Communists. We therefore returned to containment, only to find ourselves helpless to aid the embattled Hungarians in the fall of 1956, when Soviet power faced a serious crisis.

1956

The revolt in Hungary was brutally and effectively crushed, but the events of 1956 were political disasters of the first magnitude for the Soviet Union. Some believed then that the disintegration of the Communist empire was beginning. Others called it a mark of the military power and spiritual weakness of the Soviet system. Others were impressed with the fact that the workers, the intellectuals, and the students in particular had turned against the system, thus proving that the power and influence of communism had been exaggerated. In short, the 1956 revolts put the value of the disloyal area to the Soviet Union in question. Moreover, the Communist movement throughout the world suffered a kind of spiritual crisis because of this revolt and the Soviet reaction to it.

After 1956, the United States and its allies returned to their defensive and reactive containment policy, strengthening the areas most susceptible to Communist pressure; persuading the Communists that we would resist expansion by force if necessary, but would not attack the Communist states; seeking to direct the energies of the entire world toward a peaceful solution of the problems which threatened peace; and exploring new peaceful political ways of strengthening contacts and increasing influence among the peoples living in Eastern Europe. However, in 1957 and 1958, Mr. Kennan, the author of the containment doctrine, was one of those who advocated a policy known as disengagement, which suggested creation of a thinning out or "mutual withdrawal" of forces from the heart of Europe in order to reduce tension and armaments. Thus, Western and Soviet troops were to move away from the line which separated them, with the Western forces possibly evacuating all of Western Europe and the Soviet troops moving back from Eastern Germany and Czechoslovakia. This proposal was based on a false analysis of the causes of the conflict and of probable Soviet policies. Above all, it reflected the belief that the Western powers could do little to assist the peoples of Eastern Europe, whose lives and philosophies were, presumably, being permanently reshaped under Communist rule. Indeed, Mr. Kennan in 1958 wrote

> If things go on as they are today, there will simply have to be some sort of an adjustment on the part of the peoples of Eastern Europe, even if it is one that takes the form of general despair, apathy, demoralization, and the deepest sort of disillusion with the West. The failure of recent popular uprisings to shake the Soviet military domination has now produced a bitter and dangerous despondency throughout large parts of Eastern Europe. If the taste or even the hope of independence dies out in the hearts of these peoples, then there will be no recovering it; then Moscow's victory will be complete. . . . (from *Russia and the West*)

Fortunately, American policy was little affected by those who were tempted by disengagement, and the opportunities which had been seized and which are now even more full of promise have developed because of containment, the errors of the Communists, and the faith and resolution of the peoples of Eastern Europe.

*American Objectives and General Policies: Some Choices**

Most Americans agree that we should continue to seek the reduction and ultimately the withdrawal of Soviet military forces

---

* This section relies on the excellent analysis by John C. Campbell, *American Policy Toward Communist Eastern Europe*.

from Eastern Europe, the achievement by the East Europeans of self-determination and of control over their foreign policies, and the unification of Germany through free elections. Some Americans, but probably very few, believe the United States should seek to destroy communism in the Soviet Union, in Eastern Europe, and wherever it exists. Few advocate open war to achieve these goals, most believing that the Soviet Union will retreat under heavy political and military pressure, as it did in Cuba in 1962. Other Americans, also a small group, believe that the world situation is such and the perils of nuclear war so overwhelming that we should seek immediate agreement with the Soviet Union, even accepting (and forcing our allies to accept) the continued division of Germany and Europe and the maintenance of present arrangements in Eastern Europe.

The general lines of agreement and disagreement on broad lines of policy reflect the same philosophies or concepts concerning long-term objectives. Thus, those who accept the most extreme position concerning objectives urge the increase of political and economic measures, capitalizing on whatever strains afflict the Communist states and seeking to strengthen resistance. They would press on every occasion for the freedom of the peoples of Eastern Europe, would advocate increased armament and tightened alliances, would establish firm controls over trade with Communist states, would insist on political benefits for trade concessions, and would reduce or eliminate cultural exchange programs.

Those who advocate a soft line, on the other hand, would treat the states of Eastern Europe as they would the Soviet Union, i.e., they would end all efforts to assist them toward self-determination. We should therefore seek to promote the liberalization of each of the Communist states, to emphasize the common interest in peace, and to use trade and even aid and expanded cultural exchange programs to create an improved atmosphere in which one day all of the pressing problems could be peacefully resolved. Thus, we should delay pressing for increased freedom, mute our propaganda, seek arrangements which would reduce military forces on both sides, abandon trade controls, and promote cultural contacts in every way possible.

The third line of policy, which no doubt represents the view of a substantial majority, assumes that Eastern Europe is, will be, and should be different from the Soviet Union and that we should use our resources and skills to widen the differences and to emphasize the national interests of each of the states. This group believes that

American power should remain a quiet but ever-present force, and that we should use trade, and even aid, and our cultural contacts to assist each people to work its own way gradually and peacefully toward greater freedom. Above all, the United States should use its diplomacy to increase in every way possible "the freedom of maneuver and bargaining power of the Eastern European states with the Soviet Union." It should seek to quiet the fear of Germany within Czechoslovakia and Poland; it should increase the opportunities of the Eastern Europeans within various international organizations where their national interests might develop along lines different from those of the Soviet Union; and it should assist the East Europeans to become active members of Western European economic and cultural organizations.

Active or Positive Containment

The policy which the United States began to follow after 1958 or so might be called containment plus, containment supplemented, or active or positive containment. It has the same foundations as the original doctrine of 1947. It is based on the same confidence that the Soviet position will not be permanent. It also reflects the belief that there will be no sudden "violent upthrust of liberty" in Eastern Europe. In short, it commits the American people to the assumption that the revolutionary age has ended and that "peaceful engagement" offers us and Eastern Europe opportunities and advantages for advancing together toward a peace based on national self-determination and independence. It rests on the conviction that we should not apply force or pressure on the Soviet Union, but that we should rely on gradualism, on the slow growth of established and new forces, and on reconciliation between ourselves and the Soviet Union. Finally, it assumes that we should in the long run triumph in a peaceful competition of this kind, fought with the weapons of peace and under circumstances which favor states which believe in the rule of law.

In this new contest, the United States seeks to strengthen the semi-independence of the peoples of Eastern Europe and to enable them to obtain more control over their own foreign policies in such a way as not to frighten the Soviet Union but instead to contribute to the peaceful solution of problems throughout Europe. Such a policy, which will demote military power and reduce fear, will in a sense outflank the Soviet presence in Eastern Europe, especially in

Eastern Germany, and assist the peoples of Eastern Europe to achieve their goals in the only way now possible, through gradual, peaceful progress.

The two best means of demonstrating the continued American interest in their development in freedom and to "build bridges" into Eastern Europe are through expanded trade and cultural relations. As opportunities for greater contact with peoples in Eastern Europe have increased, the American government has relaxed its attitude toward trade and cultural exchange with each country, recognizing, as Secretary of State Rusk said in February 1964, that we should establish a system for "treating different Communist countries differently." The address of President Johnson in May 1964, in which he spoke of building bridges across the gulf between the West and the peoples of Eastern Europe, marked another stage in our understanding of a new approach to this critical group of problems. This policy was carried further by a speech of President Johnson in October 1966, in which he discussed opening "new relations to the countries seeking increased independence" and ensuring free play to "the powerful forces of legitimate national pride." American policy is now directed toward increasing the differences among the states of Eastern Europe and toward encouraging each one to strike out on its own to achieve its own goals and gradually to re-establish normal relations with the people of the West. In seeking to reach these objectives, the United States and its allies must make use of many instruments, of which trade and cultural exchange are only two, and by no means the most important. In fact, one of our problems is to recognize that the base of our position must remain military, economic, and political strength, continuing coordination of policy among the Western states, and resolution. We must not overestimate what can be achieved through trade and cultural exchanges. We must admit that other developments within and beyond Eastern Europe created the conditions in which expanded trade and cultural relations have become possible. We do need to recognize that splendid opportunities for peaceful development have emerged, that this is an age in which the speed of change is extraordinarily great, and that we are part of a powerful process which is carrying the entire world into different levels of political development.

CULTURAL EXCHANGE

Since 1958, the Department of State, American private foundations, particularly the Ford Foundation, American universities, and organizations such as the American Friends Service Committee, the National Academy of Sciences, and the Inter-University Committee have administered programs which have brought increasing numbers of scholars and other important leaders from the countries of Eastern Europe to the United States and have sent a significant number of American scholars and others to the countries of Eastern Europe. Thus, the Ford Foundation between 1958 and 1963 enabled approximately five hundred scholars from Poland alone to continue their studies in Western Europe or in the United States. The Inter-University Committee since 1962 has enabled more than sixty scholars from Czechoslovakia, Hungary, and Bulgaria to continue their research in the United States and has sent a similar number of Americans to study in those countries. In the first six months of 1966, more than eight hundred men and women from Czechoslovakia, Hungary, Romania, and Poland were in the United States on scientific, cultural, or academic programs of one kind or another. Fewer than one hundred Americans were in those countries—but these figures are nevertheless impressive when one recalls the years before 1956 and the impact a handful of highly talented men and women can have upon a society previously isolated.

Yugoslavia, far more open to the West and with many more opportunities for its citizens to travel, has benefited more than other Communist states from a wide range of contacts, and has also changed more. Beginning in the early 1960's, the Ford Foundation began annually to assist approximately thirty scholars from Yugoslavia and an equal number from Hungary to continue their studies in the United States. This program was designed to expand into Romania and Bulgaria and was resumed in Poland in the fall of 1967. The Fulbright program was established in November 1964 between the United States and Yugoslavia to expand the exchange of scholars and professors, and this imaginative program may also be extended into Romania, where a small program administered by the Institute of International Education for the Department of State has been the only cultural exchange. In 1966, the Inter-University Committee launched an arrangement for bringing a few scholars in the field of American studies from some of the Eastern European countries to the United States as part of an effort to inaugurate the study of American history and literature there. The National Academy of Sciences at the same time began to expand its small but significant exchange program from the Soviet Union into some of the countries of Eastern Europe as well.

Thus, the flow of scholars between the United States, particularly its universities, and the countries of Eastern Europe has expanded gradually since 1958, with profound intellectual and political influences on both sides. At the same time, the Department of State has sought successfully to widen this flow in order to reach other significant groups by facilitating the distribution of American movies; the participation of American athletes in contests in Eastern Europe; exhibits of scientific, agricultural, and medical equipment; and the increased flow of leaders in various walks of life to the United States. Even the increasing number of tourists to Eastern Europe constitutes an important part of the opening-up of that area to American and other influences, because they have helped to assure the peoples of Eastern Europe of American concern and have quietly demonstrated to them some of the advantages a free society possesses.

Radio Free Europe and the Voice of America have remained important contributors to increasing the fund of information available to Eastern Europeans and to improving the quality of their own press and radio services. In fact, the expanded knowledge which East Europeans have acquired, particularly over the radio, has helped them to expand their other freedoms. The flow of published materials into these countries is still restricted; this constitutes one of the challenges of the years ahead. American and other Western publications are readily available in Yugoslavia, and to some degree in Poland and Hungary, but the informed citizen of Eastern Europe is generally denied access to publications which constitute an important part of the intellectual substance of modern man.

The United States should show more imagination and daring in its intellectual relationships with Eastern Europe. Our government, our publishers, and our intellectuals should devise ways and means for replenishing the libraries of Eastern Europe and making Western publications more readily available. Several universities, for example, might combine to establish a university bookstore in Prague, presumably on the property of Charles University or of the Academy of Sciences, selling for local currency any and every kind of Western publication and serving at the same time as a purchasing center for those American universities interested in expanding their collections of Czechoslovak publications. Americans could and should work together with Romanians and Bulgarians on projects of mutual concern and on which each could make important contributions, such as crop yields, medical research, urbanization, air pollution, and other problems common now to all peoples. We should complete arrangements for exchanging information in areas central to the modernization process, such as business management, public administration, and non-strategic technology, to help speed the transformation already underway in Eastern Europe.

Projects of this kind, involving several men and women from this country, from one or two countries of Eastern Europe and perhaps from another state as well, should create more permanent and effective relationships than do the exchange programs. Moreover, the establishment of collaborative projects of this type should also persuade the various American organizations involved to establish a loose federal organization to ensure maximum use of our resources.

The people of Western Europe are closer, geographically and culturally, than we to the people of Eastern Europe, and their governments, universities, and private organizations have been active in the same way as we in expanding intellectual contacts with Eastern Europe. In fact, they have been somewhat more successful, because their radio—and even some of their television systems—can easily reach into Eastern Europe. Travel is easier and less expensive than it is across the Atlantic, and Danes, Bulgarians, and Italians seem less harmful to some of the Communist rulers than do Americans. In short, the United States should assist the development of increased cultural contacts between the peoples of the two halves of Europe.

The expansion of cultural exchanges with the countries of Eastern Europe since 1958 has naturally been achieved with the advice and consent of the Communist rulers of those countries. Indeed, these men, presumably devoted to their philosophy and their system of government, have aims and ambitions with regard to cultural exchange which persuade them that the increase in contact is to their advantage more than to ours. In short, our goals are quite different from those of the Communists. The great gap or conflict between our goals and theirs constitutes one of the hazards which cultural exchanges face. Perhaps even more important (particularly for those Americans who are critical of such relations with the Communist states and who accept either liberation or disengagement as more effective alternatives) is the possible moral demobilization which may result from accepting the continued existence of the Communists and from doing business with Communist countries. Some believe that this kind of relationship will not only weaken the resolution of the Western states, but will provide respectability and prestige to the Communists and will undermine and perhaps even destroy the faith of those who have been forced to live so long under Communist rule.

Moreover, while many see cultural exchange as a means of weakening and dividing the Communist states, others see it as an instrument which may boomerang and divide the West itself. Many Americans clearly lack the political sophistication to support a policy which appears weak and opportunistic. Moreover, as the Western states scramble with each other for advantages in cultural exchange and the increase in trade often associated with it, political divisions may increase. As relations become more and more relaxed, local Communist parties and friendship associations, particularly in Western Europe, may come to play a prominant role in the exchanges, diverting them from the goals we envisage and creating serious additional political hazards which may threaten the existence of the exchange. We must assume, in addition, that the scientists and other scholars sent to the West by Communist governments will acquire important knowledge of a scientific, technical, and military character, which may be far more substantial than we appreciate and which may on occasion help produce truly significant increments to Communist power. We must also assume that some of those who travel in the West on exchange programs may be agents, engaged in subverting the countries in which they are temporarily living. In other words, the Communist governments can make use of the cultural exchange program in order to increase their power and to strengthen their systems.

Perhaps the most serious threat to the expansion of cultural exchange is the possibility that the American people will not have the patience, endurance, and simple faith in themselves and in others to support a policy the results of which may come in a slow and undramatic fashion. We must remember that Mr. Kennan himself, the architect of the doctrine of containment, wrote in the spring of 1956 that "there is finality, for better or worse, about what is happening in Eastern Europe," and that his faith even after the revolts of 1956 was minimal.

Cultural relations with Communist states may raise other problems within the United States as well. For example, universities, organizations of artists and scholars, and private foundations have thus far played a prominent role in exchanges with Communist countries. The universities have been active because of their interest in expanding and improving research and instruction and because they believe that they themselves must administer any academic program in which they are engaged. They do not wish to surrender control of academic enterprises, even to a friendly and understanding government.

This sensible and necessary position may be difficult to maintain because the costs of increasing cultural exchange will almost certainly lead to greater government participation and influence. Moreover, some wonder whether universities or other such private organizations can engage in cultural exchanges with Communist governments without betraying their true interests and without destroying the qualities which have made universities in all countries the vital sources and defenders of uncompromising independence.

In summary, cultural exchanges provide the American people with an instrument for assisting the peopie of Eastern Europe, but an instrument which may be double-edged and which may also be used by the Communists to strengthen their own system. Those Americans who doubt the efficacy, and even necessity, of this approach should remember those bitter years in which the Soviet Union and the Communist states so tightly restricted relations with the rest of the world that few connections of any kind existed. The Western radio was jammed, and the Western states were reduced to sending balloons over Czechoslovakia and Poland, with leaflets being released by mechanical or chemical devices to float down upon people completely isolated otherwise from their fellowmen.

TRADE

The expansion of trade offers another opportunity to the United States, although it raises even more complicated problems. In spite of the changes which have occurred since the death of Stalin, particularly since 1956, the trade of the Eastern European countries is still tied to the Soviet Union through COMECON (Council of Economic Mutual Assistance) and long-term trade commitments. Moreover, although Eastern Germany, Czechoslovakia and Hungary are important industrialized states, the principal exports are foodstuffs, timber, coal and oil products, fabrics, clothing and footwear, and machinery and metal products. None of these products are in strong demand in the United States, and their quality is often low in any case. The principal imports of Eastern Europe—cotton, wool, heavy hides, natural rubber, copper, foodstuffs, and modern plant equipment—are all among American exports, but these products are not matched or cannot be paid for by East European exports.

In addition, the Eastern European states generally require long-term credits for financing trade. Thus, opportunities for increased trade between the United States and the countries of Eastern Europe are not very great. American exports to Eastern Europe in 1964 amounted to only $193,000,000, approximately one-tenth the volume of exports from Western Europe to Eastern Europe. In that same year, American imports from Eastern Europe amounted to only $78,000,000. In both cases, trade with Eastern Europe amounted to less than one-tenth of one per cent of the American total.

On the other hand, the trade of Western Europe, particularly Western Germany, with Eastern Europe has increased significantly since 1955 and shows great promise of growing. For example, exports from Western Europe to Eastern Europe and imports from Eastern Europe doubled between 1955 and 1964. The two halves of Europe have a natural trade relationship, because each produces materials or equipment necessary in the other. Even so, in 1966, the trade of the NATO countries with Eastern Europe amounted to only approximately three per cent of their total trade, at a time when the trade of the Eastern European countries with the NATO countries amounted to twenty per cent of their total trade. Perhaps the United States can contribute most significantly by approving and assisting in the expansion of trade between Western and Eastern Europe, especially by encouraging the admission of the Eastern European states into wider trading and other organizations, such as OECD, GATT, and the aid consortia of the World Bank, and the expansion of the availability of credit for trade from international sources.

Two or three additional steps of some significance could be adopted. Thus, the United States could enable Poland and Yugoslavia to qualify for the Food for Peace program, particularly during those years when they have special need. The Congress could pass the East-West trade bill which would authorize the President to extend the "most favored nation" advantages to the Soviet Union and Eastern Europe, reducing significantly the tariffs against which their products must compete in the American market. This would have only a minute effect upon the American economy, but would be a very substantial benefit to the countries of Eastern Europe and would thereby enable them to increase their independence from the Soviet Union. Both of these measures would raise cries of outrage among some sections of American opinion, but this serves only to identify the dilemmas which such opportunities as these inevitably raise.

Other Dilemmas

The problems involved in increasing or expanding cultural relations and trade with Western Europe are to some degree symbolic of the problems which the United States faces in dealing with that area of the world. However, others even more critical must be resolved before we can help these people make more substantial progress towards independence. Thus, the United States and its friends in Western Europe must reach some agreement concerning the role which Western European states must play with regard to Eastern Europe. France, the United Kingdom, and Italy are busy expanding or rebuilding their earlier connections with these countries. Western Germany, particularly since Kurt Kiesinger became Chancellor in the fall of 1966, has redefined its Eastern policy as the "peaceful rebuilding of our relations with the East, including an end to the German problem." Since 1960 in particular, the German Federal Republic has enormously increased its trade, especially with Hungary, Poland, Bulgaria, and Romania. It has trade missions in all of the countries of Eastern Europe, except Albania, and it arranged an exchange of embassies with Romania in early 1967.

There is and should be no conflict between the policies of our allies and our own with regard to Eastern Europe, and we should regard every strengthened tie a contribution to the general welfare. However, we should not allow our successes to dim our interests or to lead anyone to believe we are retreating from Europe. We must be alert to the strongly-felt necessity in West Germany for a continued American presence and American military aid. Indeed, for both the United States and its allies, German reunification must remain the central policy problem. The Federal Republic must continue to be confident of the support of the United States and its allies for the reunification of Germany, and all of the Western states must be alert for opportunities to advance the cause of reunity for Germany and for Europe. In particular, the United States, with the Federal Republic, should be prepared to accept the Oder-Neisse line as the boundary between Poland and a reunited Germany when the Communist powers are prepared to withdraw from the Elbe.

The United States must also assist in establishing some European or Atlantic framework in which the countries of Eastern Europe can live peacefully, without in any way alarming or threatening the Soviet

Union. No one would benefit if the states of Eastern Europe should gradually work their way free towards independence only to have no system of European states into which they could fit, thus becoming free-floating bodies in a very tense world atmosphere under circumstances which might lead them back under Soviet authority. Proposals abound, but the very proliferation of concepts illuminates the danger. For example, the European Economic Community is an important part of the Western system, but its policies raise trading problems for East European states and in fact threaten their continued economic progress. Moreover, the existence of the community may make more difficult the creation of a larger political union within which Eastern Europe could fit comfortably. Other proposals include the Atlantic partnership proposed by President Kennedy, the *Europe des patries* of General DeGaulle, the Europe from the Atlantic to the Urals of General DeGaulle, the NATO military structure, and the suggestion that an American-European-Russian community be established from San Francisco to Vladivostok.

Moreover, of course, our policies toward the peoples of Eastern Europe must be defined and executed against an international background, one which finds us seeking improved relations with Eastern Europe and the Soviet Union at the same time we oppose communist aggression in Viet Nam and other parts of the world. There is no inconsistency of purpose in these policies, which seem opposed and mutually contradictory, because both are instruments designed to promote peace and freedom. Complicated and flexible policies, such as these, will require wisdom, understanding, and support from the American people if they are to be successful.

However, our principal problem remains that of maintaining the patience, the skill, and the resolution necessary to enable us to assist the East Europeans. We are now suffering from the perils of prosperity, for the revival and the dynamism of the West have brought with them over-confidence and the disintegration of the sense of shared common purpose of the 1950's. The disarray of the West and uncertainty concerning those who would rally when the trumpet calls have increased American restlessness and dissatisfaction and revived the spectre of isolationism. We must remain faithful gardeners, rather than mechanics.

Index

G

H

The American Assembly

The American Assembly holds meetings of national leaders and publishes books to illuminate issues of United States policy. The Assembly is a national, non-partisan educational institution, incorporated in the State of New York.

The Trustees of the Assembly approve a topic for presentation in a background book, authoritatively designed and written to aid deliberations at national Assembly sessions at Arden House, the Harriman (N.Y.) Campus of Columbia University. These books are also used to support discussion at regional Assembly sessions and abroad and to evoke consideration by the general public.

All sessions of the Assembly, whether international, national, or local, issue and publicize independent reports of conclusions and recommendations on the topic at hand. Since its establishment in 1950, The American Assembly has joined almost 90 educational institutions in holding these sessions. Participants constitute a wide range of experience and competence.

American Assembly books are purchased and put to use by individuals, libraries, businesses, public agencies, nongovernmental organizations, educational institutions, discussion meetings, and service groups.

The subjects of Assembly programs to date are:

1951——United States–Western Europe Relationships
1952——Inflation
1953——Economic Security for Americans
1954——The United States' Stake in the United Nations
——The Federal Government Service
1955——United States Agriculture
——The Forty-Eight States
1956——The Representation of the United States Abroad
——The United States and the Far East
1957——International Stability and Progress
——Atoms for Power
1958——The United States and Africa
——United States Monetary Policy
1959——Wages, Prices, Profits, and Productivity
——The United States and Latin America
1960——The Federal Government and Higher Education
——The Secretary of State
——Goals for Americans

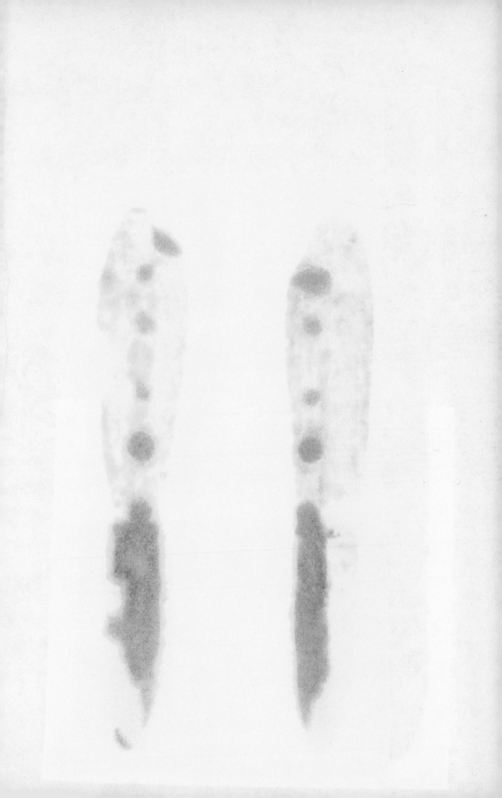

DATE DUE